circuit
hikes

in
shenandoah
national
park

potomac appalachian trail club
vienna, virginia
1996

Circuit Hikes in Shenandoah National Park

Text by
Michael Barreda

Edited by
Jean Golightly

Maps by
Dave Pierce

1996
14th Edition
POTOMAC APPALACHIAN TRAIL CLUB
118 Park Street, SE
Vienna, VA 22180

Library of Congress Number 96-67649
ISBN 0-915746-76-X

SHENANDOAH CIRCUIT HIKES

POTOMAC APPALACHIAN TRAIL CLUB
118 Park Street, SE
Vienna, VA 22180
(703) 242-0315

This guide is published by the Potomac Appalachian Trail Club (PATC). The PATC is a volunteer group whose main purpose is the preservation and maintenance of a section of the Appalachian Trail (*AT*) and other trails in the local area. The PATC is also responsible for a variety of hiking guides and maps, other publications, hiking, climbing, and ski-touring excursions, and other activities. PATC Headquarters is open Mon-Thurs from 7pm-9pm and Thurs-Fri from 12pm-2pm, except holidays. Visitors and callers are welcome.

In a guide such as this, it is inevitable that errors, both typographical and factual, will occur. Changes in trails occur regularly, so it is difficult to keep a guide current. Please report any errors or changes you may find to the editor, care of PATC, so that they may be incorporated into future editions.

Springs
The purity of water from natural sources found along trails cannot be guaranteed. All water from natural sources should be treated before use.

The Potomac Appalachian Trail Club expressly denies any liability for any accident or injury to persons using these trails.

INTRODUCTION

This edition of Circuit Hikes in Shenandoah National Park describes 31 hikes. Counting the long and short versions of the various hikes, this guide describes 42 circuits, listed in geographic order from north to south along Skyline Drive. Some of these hikes are relatively flat, others are rugged rock scrambles; some are short afternoon strolls, others are all-day, exhausting trips. Determine how many miles or how much time you want to spend on a hike, and then read the introductions to find the hike that suits your mood.

TIPS FOR HIKERS

Circuit Length—Distances are rounded to the nearest 0.1 mi. Trail distances were measured just prior to the publication of this edition; they may not agree with distances posted on trail signs that predate trail changes.

Time Estimates—Time estimates are based on a hiking speed of 2 mi/hr plus 30 min for each 1,000-ft gain in elevation. Some hikes have been corrected upwards based on the ruggedness and steepness of the terrain.

Difficulty Ratings—Ratings are based on ruggedness of trail, elevation change during hike, and overall distance traveled. This guide uses three ratings: easy, moderate, and strenuous.

Elevation Change Estimate—An elevation change estimate indicates the sum of the ascents on a circuit; it does not necessarily indicate the difference in elevation between the highest and lowest points on the circuit.

Maps—Maps are drawn to 100-ft contour intervals. For more complete maps of the Park, refer to PATC Map 9 for the North District, PATC Map 10 for the Central District, and PATC Map 11 for the South District.

Distances on Skyline Drive—Distances on Skyline Drive are identified by mileposts beside the road. This guide refers to these mileposts to locate trailheads.

Trail Signs—Signs appear and disappear from time to time. Use the map to keep track of your whereabouts and do not depend only on signs.

Itinerary—Leave your planned route and your planned time of return with someone at home. Hike with a friend.

Weather—In the mountains the weather is more extreme than at lower elevations, and it can change rapidly. Carry raingear, an extra sweater, and extra food and water. Be familiar with the symptoms and treatment of hypothermia.

Water—Carry adequate drinking water. Although streams may look clean and fresh, the water may be unsafe to drink unless treated.

Litter—No one enjoys a messy trail. Be sure to carry out everything you carry in, and please help maintain the trails by carrying out any litter you encounter.

Poisonous Snakes—Timber rattlesnakes and copperheads may be encountered on any of these hikes. These snakes are not aggressive, but they do not tolerate being approached or stepped on. Be aware of where you put your feet and hands, especially in rocky areas.

Four Hikes in One—Expand your hiking experiences by including all four seasons. Each has its own rewards.

ABBREVIATIONS

AT	Appalachian Trail
ft	feet
hr	hours
mi	miles
min	minutes
MP	Skyline Drive milepost
Mtn	Mountain
PATC	Potomac Appalachian Trail Club
SNP	Shenandoah National Park
SR	state road
yd	yards

LEGEND

Trail Blazes

Single blaze marks the trail

Double blaze means "watch for change in direction"

Roads

Paved roads

Gravel/dirt roads

Trails

• • • • • • • • • • • Appalachian Trail

Other Trail

Fire Road

Symbols

 Shelter

 Cabin

Gate

Spring

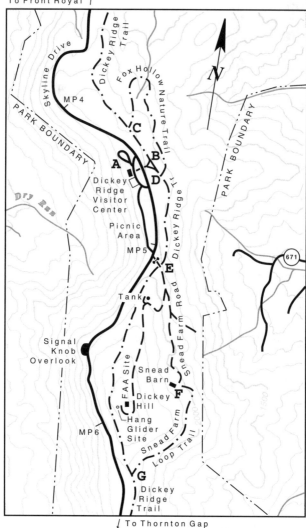

To Front Royal ↑

Skyline Drive

Dickey Ridge Trail

Fox Hollow Nature Trail

PARK BOUNDARY

MP 4

N

PARK BOUNDARY

Dry Run

C

A
B
D

Dickey
Ridge
Visitor
Center

Picnic
Area

MP 5

Dickey Ridge Trail

E

671

Tank

Snead Farm Road

Signal
Knob
Overlook

FAA Site

Snead
Barn

F

Dickey
Hill

Hang
Glider
Site

Snead Farm

MP 6

Loop Trail

G

Dickey
Ridge
Trail

↓ To Thornton Gap

0.0   0.5   1.0 Miles

Hike No. 1
FOX FARM—
SNEAD FARM LOOP

1

Length:	5.0 mi
Time Estimate:	3 hr 30 min
Difficulty:	Easy
Elev. Change:	1000 ft

Description: This circuit has well-maintained and marked trails. It descends gently through the ruins of the old Fox Farm homestead. Huge rock piles from the cleared fields, stone foundations, the Fox cemetery, old stone walls, the Snead barn, and the ruins of an old bunk house can still be seen. The circuit also offers panoramic views of Shenandoah Valley and an overlook of a hang glider launching site. **Dogs are not allowed on the Fox Hollow Nature Trail.**

Access: Go to Dickey Ridge Visitor Center, which is 0.4 mi north of MP 5 on Skyline Drive.

Directions:
[A] 0.0 Walk directly across Drive from Dickey Ridge Visitor Center to Dickey Ridge Trail map and signpost.
[B] At map and signpost, take left fork and in less than 100 yd come to concrete signpost at Dickey Ridge Trail [blue-blazed]. Turn left onto Dickey Ridge Trail and walk downhill.
[C] 0.3 Turn right at concrete signpost onto Fox Hollow Nature Trail (not blazed). Go downhill through stone remains of Fox homestead, ascend gently, then descend past Fox cemetery on left and cross seasonal wet spot. Climb short distance to sharp turn to right. Climb gently up hill in bed of

old farm road. Level out, then turn right off old road bed and climb short distance to complete loop back to Dickey Ridge Trail.

[D] 1.3 Turn left at concrete signpost onto Dickey Ridge Trail.

[E] 1.8 Turn left at signpost onto Snead Farm Road (not blazed). Avoid trail slightly uphill to right (circuit will eventually return to this point). At concrete post at first fork, take road left, downhill, and avoid road to right. At concrete post at second fork, avoid road to left and continue straight ahead, slightly uphill. At third fork, avoid road slightly uphill to right (to weather station) and remain on level road. Go past Snead barn and bunk house ruins.

[F] 2.5 At concrete signpost on left in grassy area at end of road, turn left onto Snead Farm Loop Trail [blue-blazed].

[G] 3.2 Turn right at concrete signpost onto Dickey Ridge Trail and climb. Hang glider launching area is visible where trail dips sharply left. Climb short distance to panoramic view on right, then start long descent.

[E] 4.3 Turn left onto Snead Farm Road, then immediately turn right at signpost onto Dickey Ridge Trail.

[D] 4.9 Stay left at concrete signpost at junction with Fox Hollow Nature Trail and continue 100 yd on Dickey Ridge Trail.

[B] Turn left at signpost and cross Drive.

[A] 5.0 Arrive back at Dickey Ridge Visitor Center.

Hike No. 2
BLUFF TRAIL

2

Length:	13.4 mi
Time Estimate:	7 hr 45 min
Difficulty:	Strenuous
Elev. Change:	2000 ft

Description: The Appalachian Trail presents a moderate climb as it ascends North Marshall (3368 ft) and South Marshall (3212 ft). Cliffs on North Marshall and lookout points on South Marshall offer views of surrounding peaks and valleys. A hut at Gravel Springs provides a good picnic spot. (Day use only except backpackers with permits.) The Bluff Trail is nearly level and passes through a splendid stand of forest. A side trip to Big Devils Overlook adds about one mile and is worth the effort. The trails on this circuit are in poor condition due to extensive storm damage in 1995. During late summer high weeds may be present on all trails, but hiking traffic usually keeps the paths open.

Access: Go to parking area on Skyline Drive between MP 12 and 13. Park about 50 yd north of Jenkins Gap Overlook (2355 ft) on west side of Drive (across from overlook).

Directions:

[A] 0.0 Find signpost on west side of Drive and follow yellow-blazed trail 180 ft downhill from parking area to *AT* [white-blazed]. Turn left (south) onto *AT* and climb.

0.1 Cross fire road, ascend through old apple orchard, then descend.

1.7 Cross Drive and climb *AT* steadily uphill to top of North Marshall, where trail levels. Descend from North Marshall past views to west.

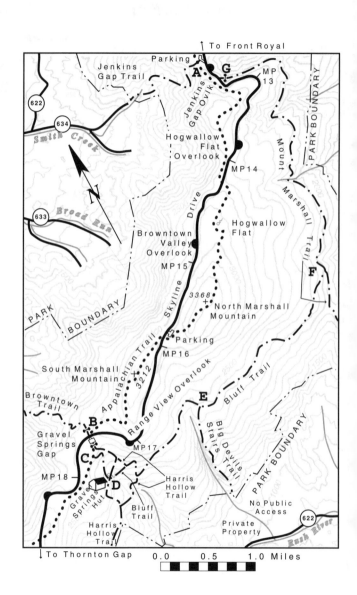

↑ To Front Royal

Parking

A **G**

Jenkins Gap Trail

Jenkins Gap Ovlk

MP 13

(622)

(634)

Smith Creek

(633)

Broad Run

Hogwallow Flat Overlook

MP14

Drive

Hogwallow Flat

F

Mount Marshall Trail

PARK BOUNDARY

Browntown Valley Overlook

MP15

Skyline

3368

North Marshall Mountain

PARK BOUNDARY

Appalachian Trail

Parking

MP16

3212

South Marshall Mountain

Range View Overlook

E

Bluff Trail

PARK BOUNDARY

Browntown Trail

B

Gravel Springs Gap

MP17

Big Devils Stairs Trail

C

MP 18

D

Harris Hollow Trail

Gravel Springs Hut

Bluff Trail

No Public Access

Private Property

(622)

Harris Hollow Trail

Rush River

↓ To Thornton Gap

0.0   0.5   1.0 Miles

3.9 Cross Drive and climb *AT* to top of South Marshall and then descend.

[B] 5.4 Pass Browntown Trail [yellow-blazed], which enters on right, and continue on *AT*. In Gravel Springs Gap (2655 ft), cross Drive to parking area. Avoid yellow-blazed fire road and follow *AT* downhill.

[C] 5.7 Turn left at concrete signpost onto Bluff Trail [blue-blazed] and follow switch backs down to Gravel Springs. Gravel Springs Hut is to right of trail.

[D] 5.9 Turn left at intersection to stay on Bluff Trail and in 80 ft pass signpost.

6.0 Where yellow-blazed Harris Hollow Trail enters on left (trails merge), continue straight, following yellow blazes.

6.1 At signpost in left-turning switchback, turn left to continue on Bluff Trail. (Harris Hollow Trail goes straight.)

[E] 7.4 Continue on yellow-blazed Bluff Trail past Big Devils Stairs Trail [blue-blazed]. (Big Devils Stairs Trail descends 0.5 mi to spectacular view from Big Devils Overlook.)

[F] 9.7 Turn left at concrete signpost onto Mount Marshall Trail [yellow-blazed].

9.9 Cross Jordan River (small stream here).

11.0 Cross Sprucepine Branch.

11.9 Cross Waterfall Branch.

[G] 13.1 Pass yellow-blazed horse trail on left and continue straight on Mount Marshall Trail.

13.2 Turn right (north) along Drive.

[A] 13.4 Pass Jenkins Gap Overlook and arrive at parking area.

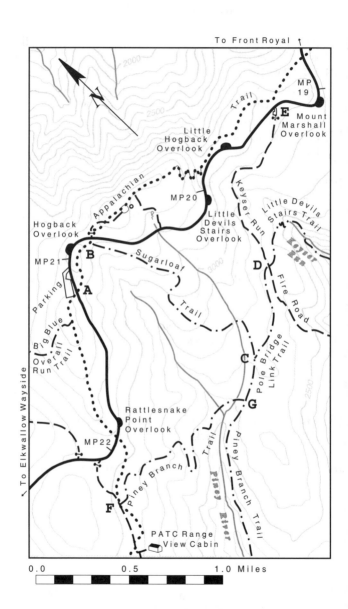

To Front Royal ↑

MP 19

Mount Marshall Overlook

E

Little Hogback Overlook

Trail

Keyser Run

Little Devils Stairs Trail

Koller Run

MP 20

Little Devils Stairs Overlook

Appalachian

Hogback Overlook

Sugarloaf

D

MP 21

B

Trail

3000

Fire Road

Parking

A

Big Blue

Overall Run Trail

C

Pole Bridge Link Trail

2500

G

Rattlesnake Point Overlook

To Elkwallow Wayside →

MP 22

Piney Branch

Trail

Piney Branch Trail

Piney River

F

PATC Range View Cabin

N

2000

2500

0.0   0.5   1.0 Miles

Hike No. 3
SUGARLOAF

	Short Circuit	**Long Circuit**
Length:	4.9 mi	9.7 mi
Time Estimate:	2 hr 45 min	5 hr 30 min
Difficulty:	Easy	Moderate
Elev. Change:	700 ft	1600 ft

Description: This circuit is a figure eight. The first half of the figure eight climbs Hogback Mountain's highest peak (3474 ft). The mountain offers a fine view of Browntown Valley, Dickey Ridge, and Massanutten Mountain from a ledge 30 ft to the right of the *AT*. The second half of the figure eight crosses Piney River and then climbs to the *AT* near Sugarloaf. (Unless the water is unusually high, crossing Piney River is not difficult.) The top of Sugarloaf offers spectacular views of Browntown Valley, Dickey Ridge, and Massanutten Mountain. Hikers who want a shorter (4.9 mi.) hike can follow the first half of the circuit's figure eight.

Access: These circuits begin on Skyline Drive at a paved area just south of Hogback Overlook and MP 21. A paved parking area large enough for ten cars is located where *AT* crosses Drive.

Directions:
- **[A] 0.0** Find *AT* where it crosses parking area and follow *AT* left (north).
- **[B] 0.3** Turn right onto Sugarloaf Trail [blue-blazed], descend a few ft, pass through mountain laurel, and cross Piney Branch.
- **[C] 1.4** Turn left onto Pole Bridge Link Trail [blue-blazed].
- **[D] 1.9** At four-way junction called Fourway, turn left onto Keyser Run Fire Road.
- **[E] 3.0** Pass gate, cross Drive, and find trail directly across from Keyser Run Fire Road. Walk 200 ft to *AT* and turn left onto *AT*.

3.5 Climb to top of Little Hogback. Fine view of Massanutten Mtn from ledge 30 ft to right of trail.

3.6 Continue on *AT* past marked spur trail that leads to Little Hogback Overlook on Drive. Veer right, descend, and then climb steeply via switchbacks up east face of Hogback Mtn to ridge crest. Continue along ridge.

4.4 Pass a few ft to left of first peak of Hogback Mtn (3420 ft).

4.5 Spur trail leads left, downhill, 0.2 mi to walled-in spring. Continue on *AT*, which begins to climb. In a few ft, pass hang glider launching area with view of Browntown Valley and Massanutten Mtn. Pass radio towers on second peak of Hogback Mtn (3474 ft). Follow tower road across turnaround area, go to right of road, and descend. *AT* crosses to left of tower road 0.1 mi later and descends.

4.6 Arrive at gate on access road to tower just before Drive.

If hiking only first half of circuit: Continue on *AT* to parking area on Drive at [A] and end of hike (4.9 mi).

If hiking entire circuit: Continue on *AT* and follow directions below.

[B] 4.7 Pass intersection with Sugarloaf Trail and continue on *AT*. Rocky outcrop 15 ft off *AT* immediately above Hogback Overlook (3440 ft) offers splendid view of Browntown Valley, Dickey Ridge, and Massanutten Mountain.)

5.2 Cross Drive to west of Hogback Overlook. In short distance pass spur trail which leads left 30 ft to fourth peak of Hogback Mtn (3,440 ft).

5.5 Pass Big Blue-Overall Run Trail, which enters from right. Descend, sometimes steeply. Outcrop on right offers views.

5.8 Cross Drive and continue on *AT*.

[F] 6.1 Turn left onto Piney Branch Trail [blue-blazed]. Descend through old apple orchard and cross Piney River.

[G] 7.6 Turn left onto Pole Bridge Link Trail [blue-blazed].

[C] 8.0 Turn left onto Sugarloaf Trail, cross Piney Branch, and ascend through mountain laurel.

[B] 9.4 Turn left (south) onto *AT* and pass gate at Hogback Overlook. Cross Drive and continue on *AT*.

[A] 9.7 Arrive at parking area to west of Hogback Overlook.

Hike No. 4
PINEY RIDGE— OVERALL RUN AREA

4

	Little Devils Stairs Circuit	**Perimeter Circuit**
Length:	5.5 mi	10.7
Time Estimate:	3 hr 45 min	6 hr 45 min
Difficulty:	Moderate	Strenuous
Elev. Change:	1800 ft	2800 ft

Description: The trails in this grouping are in an area generally bounded by Piney Ridge, the eastern Park Boundary, and Skyline Drive (between MP 19 and 23). The numerous trails and fire roads in this area offer many potential circuit hikes. The *Little Devils Stairs Circuit* climbs the steep and rocky Little Devils Stairs ravine and returns via the Keyser Run Fire Road. The sheer cliffs of the ravine are wild and picturesque, but the trail is treacherous in wet or icy weather. Many trail connections can be made using the Keyser Run Fire Road, which passes by the old Bolen cemetery near the intersection with the Hull School Trail. The *Perimeter Circuit* follows trails along the perimeter of the Piney Ridge—Little Devils Stairs area and passes the Dwyer cemetery, which contains grave sites dating from the late 1800s. The middle portion of Piney Branch Trail explores a wide ravine with two waterfalls in a deep hemlock forest. This area is frequented by bears. The trails in this area can be hiked from Skyline Drive or from the Park's eastern boundary. Directions are provided from the Park Boundary.

Access from Park Boundary: Take US 211/522 to SR 622, which is approximately 3 mi southwest of Washington, Va and 2 mi northeast of Sperryville, Va. Intersection with SR 622 is on

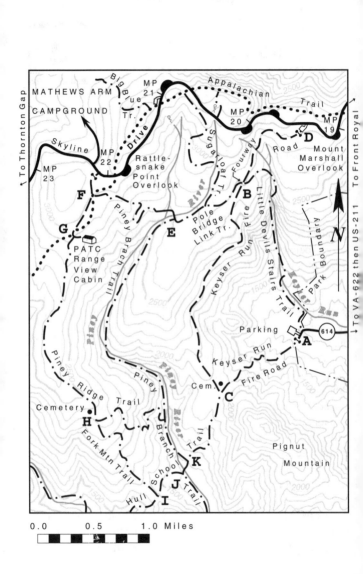

MATHEWS ARM
CAMPGROUND

Big Blue Tr.

MP 21

Appalachian

Trail

MP 20

MP 19

To Thornton Gap

Skyline

MP 22

Drive

Rattle-
snake
Point
Overlook

Sugarloaf Tr.

Fourway

D

Mount
Marshall
Overlook

MP 23

F

Piney Branch Trail

E

Pole
Bridge
Link Tr.

B

Little Devils Stairs Trail

Keyser Run Fire

N

Park Boundary

To VA-622 then US-211   To Front Royal

G

PATC
Range
View
Cabin

Keyser   Run

Piney

Parking

A

614

Piney Ridge Trail

Piney

River

Piney

Keyser Run Fire Road

Cem.

C

Cemetery

H

Fork Mtn Trail

Trail

Branch

School Trail

K

J

I

Hull

Pignut
Mountain

0.0   0.5   1.0 Miles

southwest side of highway bridge over Covington River. Follow SR 622 1.0 mi northwest toward SNP and, after approximately 2 mi, turn left onto SR 614 immediately after crossing small bridge. Follow SR 614 north for about 3 mi. (Last mile may be fairly rough.) Little Devils Stairs Trail [blue-blazed] starts from small parking area (space for about six cars) on right side of SR 614. SR 614 continues 0.1 mi to gate at Keyser Run Fire Road. **Please do not block private road.**

Access from Skyline Drive: Go to parking area 0.4 mi south of MP 19 at intersection with Keyser Run Fire Road ([D] on trail map). Pass gate on east side of Drive and hike 1.0 mi to begin circuit at [B].

Directions for Little Devils Stairs Circuit:

[A] **0.0** Follow Little Devils Stairs Trail [blue-blazed] from right side of parking area at Park Boundary.

1.0 Trail becomes steep and rocky as it climbs over boulders, crossing and recrossing Keyser Run in deep ravine.

1.7 Reach edge of ravine, veer sharply left, climb steeply, and cross site of old farm.

[B] **2.1** Where trail intersects Keyser Run Fire Road, at an intersection called Fourway, turn left onto Keyser Run Fire Road [yellow-blazed] and descend.

[C] **4.4** At concrete signpost at Hull School Trail [yellow-blazed], turn left to continue descent on Keyser Run Fire Road. (Just before this turn, walled-in Bolen cemetery is on left.)

[A] **5.5** Arrive back at parking area at Little Devils Stairs Trailhead on SR 614.

NORTH DISTRICT

Directions for Perimeter Circuit:

[A] Follow directions for *Little Devils Stairs Circuit.*

[B] 2.1 Where trail intersects Keyser Run Fire Road, at an intersection called Fourway, go straight onto Pole Bridge Link Trail [blue-blazed].

2.6 At Sugarloaf Trail, which enters on right, continue on Pole Bridge Link Trail.

[E] 3.0 Turn right onto Piney Branch Trail [blue-blazed].

3.2 Cross Piney Branch and climb.

[F] 4.4 Turn left (south) onto *AT* [white-blazed].

[G] 4.8 Pass short trail leading left to Range View Cabin. (The cabin is a locked structure available for use through advance reservations with the PATC.) Turn left onto Piney Ridge Trail [blue-blazed], which follows old roadbed. After 100 yd, turn right off road to descend on Piney Ridge Trail.

[H] 6.8 Where Piney Ridge Trail turns sharply to left, turn right onto Fork Mtn Trail [blue-blazed]. Dwyer cemetery is 100 yd before this intersection, on west side of Piney Ridge Trail.

[I] 8.1 Turn left onto Hull School Trail [yellow-blazed] and descend toward Piney Branch.

[J] 8.7 Piney Branch Trail [blue-blazed] enters on right on near side of branch. (Hull School Trail and Piney Branch Trail are concurrent here.) Bear left and ford Piney River to continue on Hull School Trail.

[K] 8.8 Turn right on Hull School Trail at intersection where Piney Branch Trail goes left.

[C] 9.6 At concrete signpost at intersection with Keyser Run Fire Road, turn right, cross gap, and descend.

[A] 10.7 Arrive back at parking area at Little Devils Stairs Trailhead on SR 614.

Hike No. 5
MATHEWS ARM— OVERALL RUN

5

	Short Circuit	**Long Circuit**
Length:	5.7 mi	9.6
Time Estimate:	3 hr 30 min	6 hr
Difficulty:	Moderate	Strenuous
Elev. Change:	1400 ft	2600 ft

Description: The trails in the Mathews Arm—Overall Run area are, for the most part, horse/foot trails [yellow-blazed] that were farm roads in pre-Park days. The Big Blue—Overall Run Trail [blue-blazed] goes to Overall Run Falls, which is spectacular when it has rained recently or in winter when it is frozen. Because both hikes begin and end at the Mathews Arm Campground, which is its highest point, they both begin with a long descent and end with a long ascent. The long circuit descends far down into Overall Run Valley and is suitable for hikers seeking a good workout. It descends along a steep and rocky path beside, and sometimes in, Overall Run and passes by several pools that are large enough for a dip. Mathews Arm Campground has been closed in recent years, but the access road to its parking lot is usually open. If the road is open, park in the campground lot. If the road is closed, park at the parking area at the intersection of the access road and the Drive and add 1.4 mi to the indicated circuit mileages. **Dogs are not allowed on the Traces Nature Trail.**

Access from Mathews Arm Campground: Go to camp's entrance road on west side of Skyline Drive, 0.2 mi south of MP 22. Descend 0.7 mi to campground registration station. Turn

right just beyond registration station and go 0.1 mi into parking area. Both hikes begin in northeast corner of this parking area.

Short Circuit Directions:
[A] **0.0** Follow Traces Nature Trail from parking area.
   0.4 At concrete signpost, follow trail right 50 yd to second concrete signpost and take right fork uphill.
[B] **0.6** At third concrete signpost, turn left onto Big Blue—Overall Run Trail [blue-blazed]. Descend, meander around swampy area known as Bearwallow, and then descend again.
[C] **2.2** Turn left onto Mathews Arm Trail [blue-blazed and yellow-blazed here].
   2.6 At Beecher Ridge Trail, which enters on right, continue left, uphill, on Mathews Arm Trail.
[D] **3.1** Turn right at concrete signpost onto Weddlewood Trail [yellow-blazed].
[I] **4.5** Take left fork at concrete signpost onto Heiskell Hollow Trail [yellow-blazed] and ascend.
[J] **5.3** Turn left at concrete signpost and follow wastewater treatment plant service road.
[A] **5.7** Arrive at Mathews Arm Campground parking area.

Long Circuit Directions:
[A] - [B]   Follow directions for *Short Circuit.*
[C] **2.2** Continue straight ahead onto Mathews Arm Trail for 100 yd and then turn left at concrete signpost to descend Big Blue—Overall Run Trail [blue-blazed]. Pass several viewpoints of Upper Falls and Big Falls and spectacular views of Massanutten Mtn. Follow steep, rocky, and often wet descent along Overall Run.
[E] **4.6** At intersection where Big Blue Trail [blue-blazed] branches right, continue straight ahead on Overall Run Trail.

4.7 Short spur trail at concrete signpost leads left to small waterfall and several "swimmin' holes." Stay on Overall Run Trail.

[F] **5.2** At concrete signpost, turn left onto Beecher—Overall Run Connecting Trail [blue-blazed]. (Overall Run Trail is not maintained beyond this point.) Ford stream and climb.

[G] **5.9** At concrete signpost, turn right (away from Beecher Ridge) onto Beecher Ridge Trail [yellow-blazed] and descend.

[H] **6.7** At concrete signpost, turn left onto Heiskell Hollow Trail and climb steadily.

[I] **8.4** At concrete signpost at junction with Weddlewood Trail [yellow-blazed], turn right to stay on Heiskell Hollow Trail and climb.

[J] **9.2** Turn left at concrete signpost and follow wastewater treatment plant service road.

[A] **9.6** Arrive at Mathews Arm Campground parking area.

Hike No. 6
KNOB MTN—
NEIGHBOR MTN AREA

6

	Jeremys Run— Neighbor Mtn Circuit	Knob Mtn— Jeremys Run Circuit
Length:	14.3 mi	12.9
Time Estimate:	8 hr 20 min	8 hr
Difficulty:	Strenuous	Strenuous
Elev. Change:	2600 ft	2900 ft

Description: Both circuits combine considerable climbs and descents with streambed hiking. The stream, Jeremys Run, is one of the most beautiful streams in the Park's North District. The circuits start at Elkwallow (2390 ft) and drop 1320 ft to the bottom of Jeremys Run, crossing the run 14 times. The *Jeremys Run—Neighbor Mountain Circuit* climbs from Jeremys Run to 2700 ft on Neighbor Mountain and then follows the *AT* back to Elkwallow. The *Knob Mountain—Jeremys Run Circuit* climbs to the peak of Knob Mountain (2865 ft), descends to Jeremys Run, and then climbs back to Elkwallow.

Access: Both circuits begin at Elkwallow Picnic Area, just south of Elkwallow Wayside near MP 24 on Skyline Drive. Park in parking area at lower end of picnic area.

Jeremys Run—Neighbor Mountain Circuit Directions:
[A] 0.0   Follow trail leading downhill from parking area. Just past comfort station, trail intersects *AT* [white-blazed]. Continue straight (south), downhill, on *AT*.

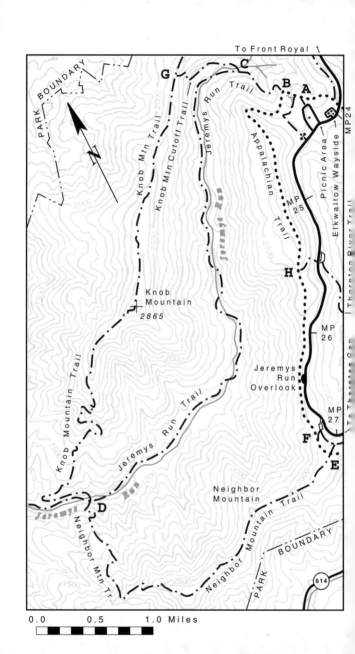

[B] **0.3** Continue straight ahead, downhill, onto Jeremys Run Trail [blue-blazed], which enters where *AT* turns left. Veer left and come within sight of Jeremys Run.

[C] **1.0** Pass concrete post at Knob Mtn Cutoff Trail [blue-blazed], which enters on right, and continue downstream on Jeremys Run Trail. Begin crossing and recrossing Jeremys Run.

5.2 Pass waterfall in Jeremys Run.

[D] **5.8** Turn left onto Neighbor Mtn Trail [yellow-blazed]. Climb via switchbacks through stands of white birch to top of ridge.

8.6 Follow trail along crest of Neighbor Mtn over several small knobs which offer views in winter.

[E] **10.4** Turn left (north), downhill, onto *AT*. Pass spur trail leading right to Drive.

[F] **10.6** Continue downhill on *AT* and begin long, steady climb.

[H] **11.9** Pass Thornton River Trail, which enters on right. (Thornton River Trail leads 0.3 mi to Drive, 0.4 mi south of MP 25.) Continue uphill, on *AT*, to high point west of Elkwallow and then descend.

[B] **14.1** Turn right (north), uphill, to stay on *AT* where Jeremys Run Trail goes left, downhill.

[A] **14.3** Where *AT* veers slightly left, continue straight ahead on spur trail. Arrive at parking area at lower end of picnic area.

Knob Mountain—Jeremys Run Circuit Directions:

[A] **0.0** Follow trail leading downhill from parking area. Just past comfort station, intersect *AT* [white-blazed]. Continue straight, downhill, on *AT*.

[B] **0.3** Continue straight ahead, downhill, onto Jeremys Run Trail [blue-blazed], which enters where *AT* turns left. Veer left and come within sight of Jeremys Run.

[C] **1.0**   At concrete post, turn right onto Knob Mtn Cutoff Trail [blue-blazed]. Descend over boulders, cross Jeremys Run, and then climb, sometimes steeply.

[G] **1.6**   Turn left onto Knob Mtn Trail [yellow-blazed], which is on fire road here.

3.7   Climb steadily to summit of Knob Mtn. Forest in this area is recovering from extensive gypsy moth damage. Just below summit, fire road ends and trail becomes footpath.

4.6   Leave crest and drop 1600 ft to Jeremys Run via many switchbacks.

[D] **7.0**   Ford Jeremys Run. Turn left, upstream, onto Jeremys Run Trail [blue-blazed]. In about 50 ft pass Neighbor Mtn Trail [yellow-blazed], which enters on right. Continue upstream on Jeremys Run Trail and begin crossing and recrossing Jeremys Run.

7.6   Pass waterfall.

[C] **11.8**   Knob Mtn Cutoff Trail [blue-blazed] goes to left. Continue straight on Jeremys Run Trail to *AT*.

[B] **12.6**   Continue straight (north), uphill, onto *AT*.

[A] **12.9**   Where *AT* veers slightly left, continue straight ahead on spur trail. Arrive at parking area at lower end of picnic area.

Hike No. 7

MATHEWS ARM— ELKWALLOW WAYSIDE

7

Length:	5.7 mi
Time Estimate:	2 hr 30 min
Difficulty:	Easy
Elev. Change:	800 ft

Description: This hike uses the Knob Mtn Trail and the Elkwallow Trail to make a pleasing circuit between Mathews Arm Campground and Elkwallow Wayside. The Wayside has a cafeteria, snack bar, camp store, and gift shop, and is open from mid-April to the end of October.

Although Mathews Arm Campground has been closed in recent years, the access road to the parking lot is usually open. If the road is closed, begin hike at Elkwallow Picnic Area.

Access from Mathews Arm Campground: Go to camp's entrance road on west side of Skyline Drive, 0.2 mi south of MP 22. Descend 0.7 mi to campground registration station. Turn right just beyond registration station and go 0.1 mi into parking area.

Access from Elkwallow Picnic Area: Go to Elkwallow Picnic Area, just south of Elkwallow Wayside near MP 24 on Skyline Drive. Park at parking area at lower end of picnic area. Follow trail downhill where sign says "To Jeremys Run and *AT*." Begin hike at [C].

Directions from Mathews Arm Campground:

[A] **0.0** Hike back to entrance road and follow Elkwallow Trail, marked by concrete post, from right (southeast) side of Mathews Arm Campground entrance road. Meander through

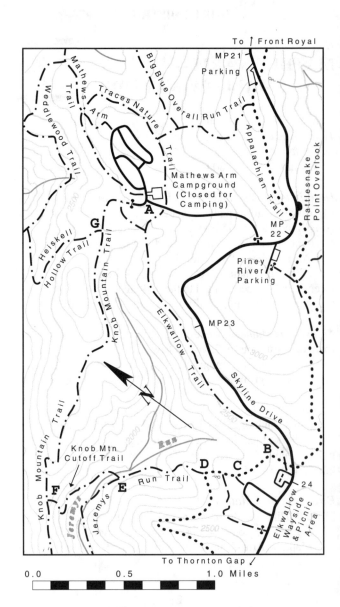

sparse woods and descend to wooden bridge. Cross bridge and climb slightly. Trail becomes level or slightly downhill.

[B] **1.5** Reach four-way intersection with *AT* [white-blazed].

To bypass Elkwallow Wayside: Turn right (south) onto *AT* and continue.

To visit Elkwallow Wayside: Continue on Elkwallow Trail straight past four-way intersection with *AT*. To return to *AT*, walk around back of Wayside building and continue straight ahead parallel to Drive. At paved Elkwallow Picnic Area road, turn right, downhill, onto road to where paved road loops left to go back up to Drive. Follow trail leading downhill from parking area. (Sign saying "To Jeremys Run and *AT*" marks this trail.)

[C] **1.8** Reach side trail that leads from *AT* to Elkwallow Picnic Area.

After bypassing Elkwallow Wayside: Continue on *AT*.
After visiting Elkwallow Wayside: Turn left (south), downhill, onto *AT*.

[D] **2.1** Continue straight ahead, downhill, at junction onto Jeremys Run Trail [blue-blazed], which enters where *AT* turns left. Veer left and come within sight of Jeremys Run.

[E] **2.9** Turn right at concrete post onto Knob Mtn Cutoff Trail [blue-blazed]. Descend over boulders, cross Jeremys Run, and then climb, sometimes steeply.

[F] **3.5** Turn right onto Knob Mtn Trail [yellow-blazed].
5.0 Wastewater treatment plant is visible on left. Continue 100 yd.

[G] **5.1** At concrete signpost, continue on Knob Mtn Trail past Heiskell Hollow Trail [yellow-blazed] to gate at Mathews Arm Campground.
5.4 Pass through circle used as RV service area.
5.5 Follow paved road as it turns right and pass camp registration station.

[A] **5.7** Arrive back at parking area.

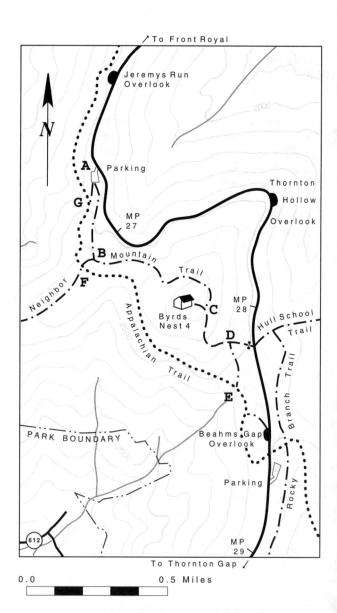

To Front Royal

Jeremys Run
Overlook

2000

N

A Parking

G

Thornton
Hollow
Overlook

MP
27

B Mountain

Trail

F

Neighbor

Appalachian

Trail

Byrds
Nest 4

C

MP
28

Hull School

Trail

D

Branch

Trail

E

PARK BOUNDARY

Beahms Gap
Overlook

2000

Parking

Rocky

612

MP
29

To Thornton Gap

0.0   0.5 Miles

Hike No. 8
BYRDS NEST NO. 4

8

Length:	2.4 mi
Time Estimate:	1 hr 30 min
Difficulty:	Easy
Elev. Change:	500 ft

Description: This short, easy circuit passes Byrds Nest No. 4 —one of the four open-faced shelters donated to the Park by the first Senator Byrd. This shelter is for day use only and makes a good spot for a picnic.

Access: Go to paved parking area on west side of Skyline Drive just north of MP 27.

Directions:
[A] 0.0 Find sign indicating Neighbor Mtn Trail and *AT*. Follow yellow-blazed Neighbor Mtn Trail (horse trail) from left side of parking area south along gentle climb. Where trail forks right, continue left.
[B] 0.3 Turn left at concrete post on Neighbor Mtn Trail [yellow-blazed] and climb to top of ridge.
[C] 0.8 After switchback to right, arrive at meadow at Byrds Nest No. 4.
    To visit shelter: Turn right to shelter.
    To continue circuit: Find shelter's access road [yellow-blazed] at lower end of meadow. Descend steeply on access road.
[D] 1.1 Turn right (north) onto blue-blazed trail at concrete post. (From this direction, no blazes are visible. Blue blazes are visible from opposite direction.)

NORTH DISTRICT

[E] **1.2** Turn right (north) onto *AT* [white-blazed] at concrete post. Pass through rocky open forest, level out, and then climb Neighbor Mtn's ridge, where trees have gypsy moth damage.

[F] **2.1** Cross Neighbor Mtn Trail [yellow-blazed] and descend on *AT*.

[G] **2.3** At concrete post, leave *AT* and take right fork onto unblazed trail—avoid trail to left that tends downward.

[A] **2.4** Arrive back at parking area.

Hike No. 9
THORNTON HOLLOW

9

Length:	13.4 mi
Time Estimate:	7 hr 45 min
Difficulty:	Strenuous
Elev. Change:	1100 ft

Description: This circuit passes through many reminders of the people who inhabited these mountains before the Park was established. It passes through some old homesteads, the remains of a Model A Ford, and the Dwyer cemetery, which contains grave sites dating from the early 1800s. In early spring the lower end of Thornton River Trail has a profusion of flowering redbud. This circuit can be hiked from either the Park's eastern boundary or from Skyline Drive. Directions are provided from the Park Boundary.

Access from Park Boundary: Go 1.0 mi north of Sperryville, Va on US 211. Immediately north of bridge over North Fork of Thornton River, turn west onto SR 612. Follow SR 612, which merges with SR 600 in about one mile. In another mile, bear left to stay on SR 612 when SR 600 continues straight ahead. At 3.18 mi, pass SR 653, which enters on right, and go to gate at Park Boundary. Only a few parking spaces are along road near Park Boundary. **Please do not block road or private driveways near Park Boundary.**

Access from Skyline Drive: Go 0.4 mi south of MP 25 and find Thornton River Trail where it crosses Drive ([C] on trail map). Begin circuit at [C] and ascend from west side of Drive. Upon reaching [B], turn right onto Thornton River Trail and return to [C]. (Circuit length from Drive is 10.6 mi.)

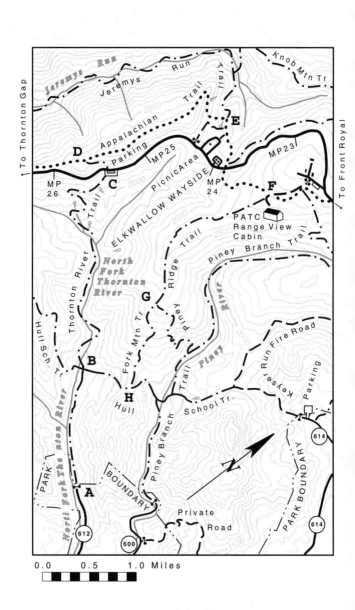

NORTH DISTRICT

Directions:

[A] **0.0** Follow Thornton River Trail [yellow-blazed] from parking area at Park Boundary. Spring is to right of road just beyond Park Boundary gate. North Fork of Thornton River is on left.

[B] **1.4** Pass Hull School Trail [blue-blazed]. Blazes on Thornton River Trail change from yellow to blue. Hike along North Fork of Thornton River, crossing river four times. Valley is wide here, with many indications of old homesteads, old roads and a Model A Ford. As valley narrows, climb gently but steadily upward through open woods.

[C] **4.2** Cross Drive diagonally to left and climb via switchbacks.

[D] **4.5** Turn right (north) onto *AT* [white-blazed] and hike through stand of evergreens.

[E] **6.7** At junction with Jeremys Run Trail [blue-blazed], turn sharply right to stay on *AT* and start gentle climb. Bear left at both forks. (First fork right leads to Elkwallow Picnic Area, second fork right leads to Elkwallow Wayside.)

7.3 Pass Elkwallow Trail [blue-blazed] and stay on *AT* 100 ft to Drive. Cross Drive and climb gradually as trail bears left.

[F] **8.1** Turn right onto Range View Cabin service road. Hike a few yd, and turn right again onto Piney Ridge Trail [blue-blazed]. (Service road continues short distance to Range View Cabin and spring 30 yd in front of cabin. This cabin is a locked structure available for use through advance reservations with the PATC.) Descend on Piney Ridge Trail.

[G] **10.1** Continue straight onto Fork Mtn Trail [blue-blazed] where Piney Ridge Trail turns sharply to left. (Old cemetery is on right 100 yd before this intersection.)

[H] **11.3** Turn right onto Hull School Trail [yellow-blazed].

[B] **12.0** Turn left onto Thornton River Trail [yellow-blazed to left, blue-blazed to right] and follow yellow blazes.

[A] **13.4** Arrive back at parking area.

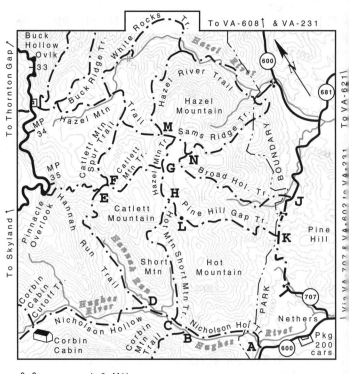

Hike No. 10
HAZEL COUNTRY

10

	Pine Hill Gap—Broad Hollow	Nicholson Hollow—Hot-Short Mtn
Length:	5.8 mi	9.9 mi
Time Estimate:	3 hr 45 min	6 hr
Difficulty:	Moderate	Strenuous
Elev. Change:	1600 ft	2000 ft

Description: Hazel Country is a region of the Park between Hazel River and Hughes River. This area contains a complex network of trails which are mostly old farm roads. The few abandoned houses which remain standing, lonely chimneys, old apple orchards, decaying split-rail fences, stone fences, and pine-forested fields are reminders of the "mountaineers" who once lived here. The *Pine Hill Gap—Broad Hollow Circuit* is a generally easy hike that passes several old log cabins. The *Nicholson Hollow—Hot-Short Mountain Circuit* has two difficult stream crossings and a steep, rough climb up Catlett Mountain.

Access to Pine Hill Gap—Broad Hollow Circuit: Take US 522 to SR·231, which is 0.8 mi south of Sperryville, Va and 12.7 mi north of Madison, Va. Go south 3.3 mi on SR 231. Just before bridge over Hazel River, turn right onto SR 681. Follow SR 681 past point where SR 600 enters on right to hard jog left at top of steep climb (2.5 mi from SR 231) at gate across Weakley Hollow Road. Park near concrete post and blue blazes on right that mark Broad Hollow Trail. **Please do not block private driveway.**

Access to Nicholson Hollow—Hot-Short Mountain Circuit: Take US 522 to SR 231, which is 0.8 mi south of Sperryville, Va and

12.7 mi north of Madison, Va. Go south 8.3 mi on SR 231, cross Hughes River, and immediately turn right (west) onto SR 602. Follow road, staying on left side of Hughes River. Route number changes to 601, 707, and then 600. Do not cross Hughes River. After 3.5 mi from SR 231, just beyond Nethers, Va, SNP parking area for 200 cars is at junction of SR 600 and Weakley Hollow Road (parking fee is charged). Nicholson Hollow Trail [blue-blazed] is 0.5 mi ahead on right (limited parking available here). **If you do not park in parking area, please be sure to park your car completely off pavement or it may be towed.**

Pine Hill Gap—Broad Hollow Circuit Directions:
- **[J]** **0.0** Hike up SR 681, past end of state maintenance. Road turns rocky and follows Park Boundary (red blazes). Climb to Pine Hill Gap and descend a few yd.
- **[K]** **0.5** At concrete post turn right onto Pine Hill Gap Trail [yellow-blazed] and climb.
- **[L]** **2.2** Turn right at concrete post onto Hazel Mtn Trail [yellow-blazed].
- **[H]** **2.5** Pass Hot-Short Mtn Trail [blue-blazed], which enters on left at concrete post, and continue on Hazel Mtn Trail.
- **[G]** **3.0** Pass Catlett Mtn Trail [blue-blazed], which enters on left at concrete post, and continue on Hazel Mtn Trail.
- **[M]** **3.5** Turn right at concrete post onto Sams Ridge—Broad Hollow Trail [blue-blazed]. Hazel School, which served this area before SNP was established, stood near this site. Spring is 200 ft downhill to right of this junction.
- **[N]** **3.7** At concrete post where Sams Ridge Trail and Broad Hollow Trail split, bear right and follow Broad Hollow Trail to begin 1400-ft descent to SR 681.
  4.4 Pass roofless cabin on left.
  4.8 Pass ruined cabin with shingled sides on right.

CENTRAL DISTRICT

5.1 Two old trails, about 250 ft apart, lead right to remains of two log buildings. Descend steeply with several sharp turns, then cross Broad Hollow Run three times.

[J] **5.8** Arrive back at SR 681.

Nicholson Hollow—Hot-Short Mountain Circuit Directions:

[A] **0.0** Hike up SR 600 to concrete post at fork where SR 600 and access to Old Rag parking area split. Continue 50 yd up SR 600 and turn right onto Nicholson Hollow Trail [blue-blazed]. Cross Brokenback Run and Hughes River. Both crossings are difficult and may require wading. Pass Park Boundary and climb.

[B] **1.2** Pass Corbin Mtn Trail [blue-blazed], which enters on left, and continue on Nicholson Hollow Trail.

[C] **1.7** Continue past Hot-Short Mtn Trail [blue-blazed] on Nicholson Hollow Trail and ford Hannah Run.

[D] **1.9** At concrete post, turn right onto Hannah Run Trail [blue-blazed]. Enormous hemlock trees grow near this trail junction. Cross small stream and climb. Ascend along Hannah Run but do not cross it.

3.4 Pass between ruins of cabins. Spring and old apple orchard are on right.

3.6 Pass ruins of cabin on left and then descend into ravine.

3.7 Cross Hannah Run. Climb is extremely steep (500 ft in 0.2 mi) and rough.

[E] **4.3** At concrete post in deep hollow, turn right onto Catlett Mtn Trail [blue-blazed]. Continue in old roadbed

[F] **4.4** Concrete post marks intersection of Catlett Mtn Spur Trail [blue-blazed] and Catlett Mtn Trail. Turn right to continue on Catlett Mtn Trail. Bear right around pit and pass remnants of stone wall on right. Hike across shoulder of Catlett Mtn and descend gently through pine and abandoned orchard. Cross stream and climb.

33

[G] **5.5** At concrete post, turn right onto Hazel Mtn Trail [yellow-blazed].

[H] **6.1** Turn right at concrete post onto Hot-Short Mtn Trail [blue-blazed] and descend.

6.2 Pass free-standing chimney about 100 ft to left.

6.7 Cross stream and continue through overgrown apple orchard.

6.9 Cross stream again. After steep descent and sharp right, descend along stream and then cross it. In about 200 ft, notice old homestead across stream to left.

8.1 Rock outcropping offers splendid view of Corbin and Robertson Mtns across Nicholson Hollow. Continue descent along old roadbed, passing between stone walls.

[C] **8.3** At concrete post, turn left onto Nicholson Hollow Trail [blue-blazed] and hike downstream toward SR 600.

8.7 Pass concrete post at Corbin Mtn Trail, which enters on right, and continue on Nicholson Hollow Trail.

[A] **9.9** Ford Hughes River, then Brokenback Run, and arrive back at SR 600.

Hike No. 11
STONY MAN MOUNTAIN

11

Length:	3.4 mi
Time Estimate:	1 hr 45 min
Difficulty:	Easy
Elev. Change:	300 ft

Description: This is one of the most scenic circuits in the Park. The trails are well maintained and marked and the grades are not difficult. The panoramic views from Stony Man and Little Stony Man are outstanding. From 1845 to the turn of the century, a copper mine operated near the summit of Stony Man. Although Stony Man Mountain (4011 ft) is the second highest peak in the Park, the climb from the parking lot is only about 330 ft. The Passamaquoddy Trail was laid out by George Freeman Pollock, founder of Skyland, in 1932. (Passamaquoddy is a Maine Indian word meaning "abounding in pollock.") This circuit can be accessed from either of two points on Skyline Drive that are two miles apart. Directions are provided from the southern access point. **Dogs are not permitted on the Stony Man Nature Trail except with long-distance AT hikers.**

Access from south: Go to northern entrance of Skyland, just south of MP 41 on west side of Skyline Drive. Turnoff to Skyland is at highest point on Drive (3680 ft). Turn into Skyland and park in Stony Man Nature Trail Parking Area on right.

Access from north: Go to Little Stony Man Parking Area, which is just south of MP 39 on west side of Skyline Drive. This parking area ([G] on trail map) only accommodates a few cars. Take spur trail from lower end of parking area to *AT* [white-

To Thornton Gap

Appalachian

MP39

Stony Man Parking

G

Skyline Drive

Trail

Little
Stony
Man

View

Cliff

D

Appalachian Trail

Hemlock
Springs
Overlook

Passamaquoddy Trail

Stony Man
4011

View

C

B

Skyland
Fire Road

*Furnace
Spring*

E

Nature
Trail
Parking

A

Skyland - Big Meadows

Horse Trail

Office &
Dining Room

SKYLAND

Water
Tank

MP42

Bushytop Trail

Skyline Drive

Stable

To Big Meadows

0.0

N

0.5 Mile

blazed] and turn left. Begin circuit at [D]. (Circuit length from north is 4.2 mi.)

Directions:

[A] **0.0** Start at Stony Man Nature Trail Parking Area. Follow Nature Trail [white-blazed] northward from right side of parking area. Nature Trail coincides with *AT* here.

[B] **0.4** Where Nature Trail and *AT* split, continue straight ahead on Nature Trail [now blue-blazed] 250 ft.

[C] At summit loop trail, turn either direction to take loop around summit and return to intersection of Nature Trail and *AT*. Summit loop trail is 0.4 mi circuit around summit of Stony Man, where cliffs offer incredible views. Continue to cliffs on blue-blazed trail. At south end of loop, spur trail [yellow-blazed] connects to Stony Man Horse Trail, which leads back to parking area.

[B] **1.1** At intersection of Nature Trail and white-blazed *AT*, turn left (north) onto *AT* and descend.

1.7 Excellent view from cliffs of Little Stony Man.

[D] **1.9** Turn left onto Passamaquoddy Trail [blue-blazed]. Follow ledge with excellent views below cliffs, pass through huge hemlocks, and continue along rugged western slope of Stony Man.

2.3 Cross first of two treacherous rock slides. Beware of loose rocks.

[E] **2.9** Pass Furnace Spring (not accessible). Continue to Skyland service road, which enters on right and continues uphill to Skyland. Turn left onto service road for 30 ft and then immediately turn left onto Stony Man Horse Trail [yellow-blazed]. Pass telephone pole and overhead power lines, then ascend gently on narrow trail.

[A] **3.4** Arrive back at Stony Man Nature Trail Parking Area.

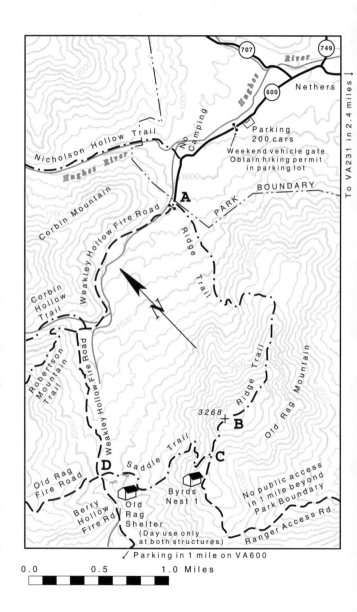

Hike No. 12
OLD RAG MOUNTAIN

12

Length:	7.1 mi
Time Estimate:	5 hr 15 min
Difficulty:	Strenuous
Elev. Change:	2200 ft

Description: Old Rag Mountain (3291 ft) is the most spectacular mountain in the northern Virginia Blue Ridge. Unlike most of the mountains in the Blue Ridge, it stands alone as an outlying mountain rather than as part of a continuous chain. Old Rag is a popular hike in all seasons; on weekends it can be crowded. Old Rag's attractions include a rugged scramble over and through boulders on the Ridge Trail and spectacular views in all directions. In spring the mountain offers displays of wild flowers, trilliums, dogwood, and redbud. This circuit includes two shelters with fireplaces that can be used for cooking: Byrds Nest No. 1 and Old Rag Shelter. Camping is not permitted at either shelter. No camping is permitted on the mountain above 2500 ft. This hike is strenuous and hikers should carry water. **Dogs are not permitted on the Ridge Trail or the Saddle Trail.**

Access: Take US 522 to SR 231, which is 0.8 mi south of Sperryville, Va and 12.7 mi north of Madison, Va. Go south 8.3 mi on SR 231, cross Hughes River, and immediately turn right (west) onto SR 602. Stay on left side of Hughes River. Route number changes to 601, 707, and then 600. Do not cross Hughes River. After 3.5 mi from SR 231, just beyond Nethers, Va, an SNP parking area accommodates 200 cars. Park here and walk 0.8 mi to small parking area at end of SR 600. A $3.00 permit fee will be charged for each person over 16. When lot is full, no more permits will be issued.

CENTRAL DISTRICT

Directions:

[A] **0.0** Start at small parking area at end of SR 600. Turn left onto Ridge Trail [blue-blazed] and climb through forest.

2.2 Come out into open, rocky area. Follow trail over, under, and around boulders, squeeze through cracks in rock, and go through tunnel in rocks.

[B] **3.3** Reach summit. Ridge Trail turns into Saddle Trail at concrete post. After exploring summit, return to this point. To continue down mountain, follow Saddle Trail [blue-blazed].

[C] **3.8** At signpost just before Byrds Nest No. 1, turn right and follow Saddle Trail. (Ragged Run Fire Road, to left, is closed to hikers at Park Boundary.)

4.1 Turn sharply right to leave ridge and descend steadily by switchbacks.

4.9 When Old Rag Shelter comes into view (100 ft ahead), turn right onto blue-blazed access road and descend. Small spring is downhill from front of shelter.

[D] **5.3** Signpost marks junction of three yellow-blazed fire roads—Weakley Hollow, Berry Hollow, and Old Rag. Turn right onto Weakley Hollow Fire Road and descend.

6.4 Pass Robertson Mtn Trail and Corbin Hollow Trail, which come in from left.

6.6 Cross large metal footbridge.

7.6 Cross series of footbridges over small stream.

[A] **7.7** Arrive back at parking area at end of SR 600.

Hike No. 13
CEDAR RUN—
WHITEOAK CANYON

13

	Short Circuit	**Long Circuit**
Length:	8.2 mi	9.6 mi
Time Estimate:	6 hr	6 hr 30 min
Difficulty:	Strenuous	Strenuous
Elev. Change:	2900 ft	3200 ft

Description: These circuits go through two of the deepest and steepest ravines in SNP, with a considerable elevation change from top to bottom. Both ravines have views of waterfalls, cascades, and high cliffs. The waterfalls are especially spectacular in winter when they are covered in ice. The circuits descend Cedar Run Canyon and ascend Whiteoak Canyon. The *Long Circuit* leads through the Limberlost, a beautiful forest of virgin hemlock. These circuits can be hiked from either the Park's eastern boundary or from Skyline Drive at the Hawksbill Parking Area, just south of MP 45. Directions are provided from the Park Boundary. **Dogs are not permitted on the Limberlost Trail.**

Access from Park Boundary: Follow SR 231 to SR 670. (This junction is about 5 mi north of Madison, Va.) Turn west onto SR 670 and pass through Criglersville, Va. About 5 mi beyond Criglersville, at Syria, Va, turn right onto SR 643. In 0.8 mi, turn left onto SR 600. (This intersection can also be reached by following SR 231 to Etlan, Va, which is about 10 mi south of Sperryville, Va, and then turning west onto SR 643 to SR 600, in about 4 mi.) Follow SR 600 (Berry Hollow Road) north, along Robinson River, for 3.6 mi. Just beyond point where road fords Cedar Run, turn left into large parking area divided into two sections by low water bridge. Whiteoak Canyon Trailhead is at end of parking area farthest from SR 600.

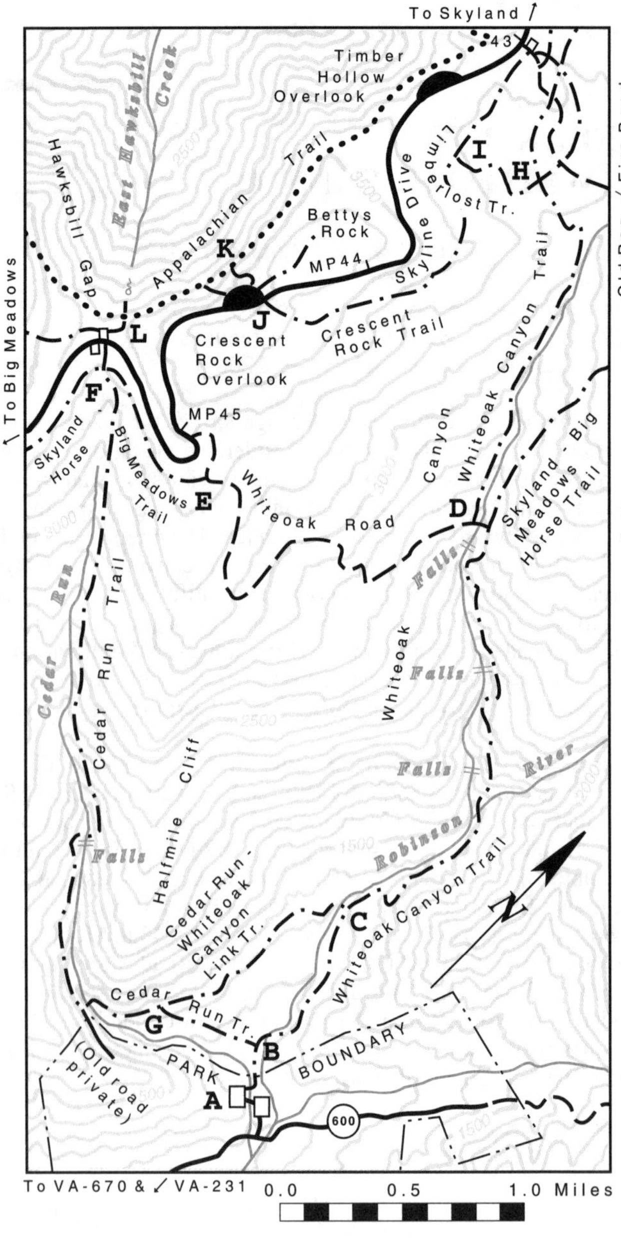

To Skyland
43
Timber Hollow Overlook
East Hawksbill Creek
Hawksbill Gap
Appalachian Trail
Limberlost Tr.
I
H
Bettys Rock
K
MP44
Skyline Drive
Old Rag Fire Road
To Big Meadows
J
L
Crescent Rock Overlook
Crescent Rock Trail
F
MP45
Whiteoak Canyon Trail
Skyland Horse
Big Meadows Trail
E
Whiteoak Road
Whiteoak Canyon
D
Skyland - Big Meadows Horse Trail
Falls
Cedar Run
Cedar Run Trail
Whiteoak
Halfmile Cliff
Robinson River
Cedar Run - Whiteoak Canyon Link Tr.
C
Whiteoak Canyon Trail
Cedar Run Tr.
G
B
PARK BOUNDARY
(Old road private)
A
600
N
To VA-670 & VA-231
0.0
0.5
1.0 Miles

CENTRAL DISTRICT

Access from Skyline Drive: Park at Hawksbill Gap Parking Area, just south of MP 45. Cross Drive and begin circuit at [F] on Cedar Run Trail. At [B], turn left to ascend Whiteoak Canyon.

Short Circuit Directions:
- **[A] 0.0** Start at parking area just off SR 600 and follow Whiteoak Canyon Trail [blue-blazed]. Cross bridge over Cedar Run.
- **[B] 0.1** Pass Cedar Run Trail [blue-blazed], which enters on left, and ford Whiteoak Run.
- **[C] 0.7** Cedar Run—Whiteoak Canyon Link Trail [blue-blazed] enters on left. Continue climbing on Whiteoak Canyon Trail. Come quite close to Whiteoak Run.

  1.4 Cross small creek, Negro Run, that enters on right.

  1.5 Falls on Negro Run are visible from trail. Begin steep ascent and remain on northeast side of Whiteoak Run. Occasional views of waterfalls are visible as trail switchbacks up canyon.

  2.7 Spur trail on left leads 250 ft to base of uppermost falls in Whiteoak Canyon.

  2.8 Excellent viewpoint to left of trail overlooks upper Whiteoak Falls.
- **[D] 2.9** Turn left onto Skyland—Big Meadows Horse Trail [yellow-blazed] and ford Whiteoak Run. (If creek is too high to cross without wading, continue upward a few yd on Whiteoak Canyon Trail, cross over footbridge, and return to horse trail.) Horse trail follows Whiteoak Fire Road.
- **[E] 4.4** At fork where horse trail goes left and fire road goes right, turn left and continue on Skyland—Big Meadows Horse Trail.
- **[F] 5.1** Turn sharply left onto Cedar Run Trail [blue-blazed] and descend into ravine.

  6.2 Uppermost waterfall on Cedar Run is visible to right.

  6.6 Ford stream and climb opposite bank of ravine.

  6.7 Approach Cedar Run again. Tallest cascade on Cedar Run is visible to left and sheer Halfmile Cliffs are visible across creek.

7.5 Turn left and ford Cedar Run immediately below falls. (Old road continues straight along stream onto private property.)

[G] 7.7 At fork, bear right to continue on Cedar Run Trail; Cedar Run—Whiteoak Canyon Link Trail [blue-blazed] enters on left.

[B] 8.1 Turn right onto Whiteoak Canyon Trail [blue-blazed], cross bridge over Cedar Run, and continue.

[A] 8.3 Arrive at parking area just off SR 600.

Long Circuit Directions:

[A] - [C] Follow directions for *Short Circuit*.

[D] 2.9 Continue on Whiteoak Canyon Trail, cross footbridge, and turn right to continue up Whiteoak Run.

[H] 4.3 Turn left onto Limberlost Trail [blue-blazed].

[I] 4.6 Turn left onto Crescent Rock Trail [blue-blazed]. (This intersection is 50 ft before boardwalk on Limberlost Trail.)

[J] 5.7 Cross Drive at Crescent Rock Overlook and follow entrance road downhill to parking area. At parking area, take Bettys Rock Trail a few ft north of overlook, turn left, and descend. (Bettys Rock is outcrop 0.3 mi ahead that offers excellent views to west. Bettys Rock Trail ends at outcrop.)

[K] 5.9 Turn left (south) onto *AT* [white-blazed].

[L] 6.3 At concrete post, turn left, uphill, onto spur trail to Drive. **6.4** Arrive at Hawksbill Gap Parking Area. Cross Drive at parking area, follow Cedar Run Trail [blue-blazed], and descend.

[F] 6.5 Cross Skyland—Big Meadows Horse Trail [yellow-blazed] and descend into Cedar Run Canyon on Cedar Run Trail [blue-blazed].

7.5 Uppermost waterfall on Cedar Run is visible to right.

8.0 Ford stream and climb opposite bank of ravine.

8.1 Approach Cedar Run again. Tallest cascade on Cedar Run is visible to left and sheer Halfmile Cliffs are across creek.

8.9 Turn left and ford Cedar Run immediately below falls. (Old road continues straight along stream onto private property.)

[G] - [A] **9.1** Follow directions for *Short Circuit*.

Hike No. 14
FREE STATE

14

Length:	4.1 mi
Time Estimate:	2 hr 30 min
Difficulty:	Moderate
Elev. Change:	1100 ft

Description: The Free State area offers a glimpse of the "mountaineer" way of life before the Park's establishment. The inhabitants in this area were very poor and fiercely independent. They were so feared by the valley folk that even sheriffs and deputies avoided entering Nicholson Hollow. The circuit passes Corbin Cabin, once the home of George Corbin and typical of mountaineer cabins in pre-Park days. The cabin has been restored by the PATC and is available for use through advance reservation. The path down to the cabin is a smooth downhill, but the trail back up to Skyline Drive is quite steep, rising 1000 ft in 1.5 mi.

Access: Go to parking area just north of MP 38 on west side of Skyline Drive.

Directions:
- [A] **0.0** From parking area just north of MP 38, walk a few ft west to *AT*. Turn left (south) onto *AT* [white-blazed].
- [B] **0.7** Turn left at concrete post onto Crusher Ridge Trail [blue-blazed]. Turn left at next concrete post onto Nicholson Hollow Trail [blue-blazed].
- [C] **0.8** Cross Drive diagonally to left and find continuation of Nicholson Hollow Trail. Descend on Nicholson Hollow Trail along old road through area of scrub oak and laurel.
  - **1.1** To right of trail is walled-in Dale Spring.
  - **2.3** Cross Indian Run.

45

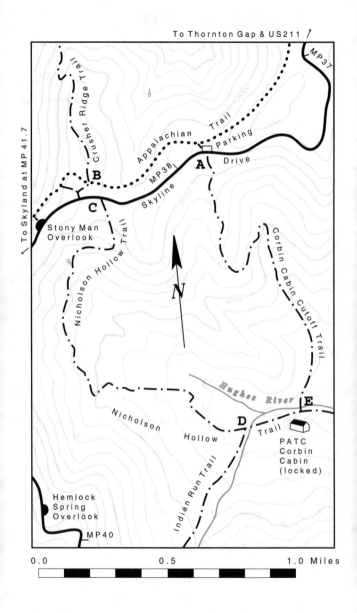

CENTRAL DISTRICT

[D] 2.6 Pass Indian Run Trail [blue-blazed], which enters on right in hemlock forest, and continue on Nicholson Hollow Trail.

[E] 2.7 Corbin Cabin is on right. Just past front of cabin, turn left onto Corbin Cabin Cutoff Trail and cross Hughes River, which is only small branch here.

3.3 Trail becomes steep and rough and then switchbacks left.

[A] 4.1 Arrive back at parking area just north of MP 38 on Drive.

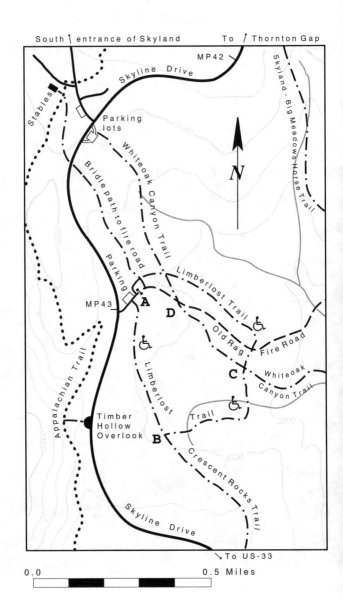

Hike No. 15
LIMBERLOST

15

Length:	1.3 mi
Time Estimate:	45 min
Difficulty:	Easy
Elev. Change:	150 ft

Description: This circuit passes through Limberlost, a beautiful forest of towering virgin hemlocks and spruces. George Freeman Pollock, the founder of Skyland, preserved these majestic trees by paying local "mountaineers" a dollar for each one they did not cut down, a considerable sum in those days. Freeman named this area for its resemblance to the forest in Gene Stratton Porter's novel, *Girl of the Limberlost*. **Dogs are not permitted on the Limberlost Trail.**

Access: Go to MP 43 on Skyline Drive and turn east onto Old Rag Fire Road (unpaved). Descend about 0.1 mi to Limberlost Parking Area.

Directions:
- **[A] 0.0** Follow Limberlost Trail, which is gravel trail to right of concrete post at southeast side of Limberlost Parking Area. Parallel Drive and pass through old farm fields.
- **[B] 0.5** Turn left to stay on Limberlost Trail where Crescent Rock Trail enters on right.
- **[C] 0.9** Turn left onto Whiteoak Canyon Trail [blue-blazed].
- **[D] 1.0** Turn left onto Old Rag Fire Road [yellow-blazed].
- **[A] 1.3** Go through yellow gate across road and arrive back at Limberlost Parking Area.

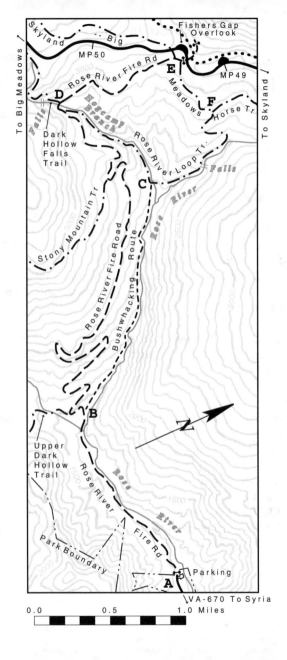

Hike No. 16
ROSE RIVER

16

	Short Circuit	**Long Circuit**
Length:	10.2 mi	12 mi
Time Estimate:	6 hr	7 hr
Difficulty:	Strenuous	Strenuous
Elev. Change:	1700 ft	2000 ft

Description: One of the main attractions of these circuits is a short (1.8 mi) bushwack along the Rose River, a good-sized stream which tumbles down ledges and boulders that form falls, cascades, and pools all along the route. Another attraction is a side trip to Dark Hollow Falls. The *Long Circuit* passes the Rose River Falls. **The bushwacking is not difficult, but novice hikers should not expect any kind of marked trail—hikers have to select their own path.**

Access: Follow SR 231 to SR 670. (This junction is about 5 mi north of Madison, Va and about 15 mi south of Sperryville, Va.) Turn west onto SR 670 and pass through Criglersville, Va. About 5 mi beyond Criglersville, go through Syria, Va. Continue on SR 670 past SR 648. Rose River Parking Area is at end of SR 670, 1.6 mi past SR 648. (For hikers coming from the north, SR 670 can also be reached by following SR 631 south 10 mi from Sperryville to Etlan, Va. Turn west at Etlan on SR 643 to Syria and SR 670.) Parking area has limited space. If parking area is full, find space back down road. Please do not block private drives.

CENTRAL DISTRICT

Directions for Short Circuit:

[A] **0.0** From parking area on SR 670, hike up road past Park Boundary onto Rose River Fire Road [yellow-blazed]. Rose River is to right in deep gorge.

1.2 Cross bridge over Dark Hollow Creek.

[B] **1.3** Where fire road turns sharply left, away from Rose River, turn right off fire road and bushwack upstream along river. (Keep close to river for scenic and easily traveled bushwacking.) A few unmarked trails turn right off fire road here and run parallel to river. (If you miss sharp left turn in fire road, you will reach Dark Hollow Trail [yellow-blazed], which enters on left.)

3.2 Rose River forks. Hogcamp Branch enters on left, Rose River continues on right. Stay to left of Hogcamp Branch and continue bushwacking.

[C] **3.5** Turn left onto Rose River Loop Trail (**do not** take unblazed trail that leads away from stream). To right, Rose River Loop Trail [blue-blazed] crosses Hogcamp Branch (on metal bridge).

[D] **4.4** Reach concrete post at Rose River Fire Road [yellow-blazed].

To make 0.3 mi side trip to Dark Hollow Falls: Turn right at junction of Rose River Loop Trail and Rose River Fire Road. Cross bridge over Hogcamp Branch, turn left onto Dark Hollow Falls Trail [blue-blazed], and go 0.2 mi to falls.

To continue circuit: Turn left onto Rose River Fire Road and descend.

5.2 Pass Stony Mtn Trail [yellow-blazed], which enters on right, and continue on Rose River Fire Road.

5.7 Pass concrete post and continue descending.

8.8 Pass concrete post at Upper Dark Hollow Trail [yellow-blazed] and continue on Rose River Fire Road.

[A] **10.2** Arrive back at parking area on SR 670.

CENTRAL DISTRICT

Directions for Long Circuit:

[A]- [B]   Follow directions for *Short Circuit*.

[C]   **3.5**   Turn right onto Rose River Loop Trail and cross Hogcamp Branch. In 250 ft cross small stream on metal bridge and in another 50 ft pass footpath leading left, uphill, to site of old copper mine. Approach main branch of Rose River.

4.0   Signpost points right to falls. To continue hike, stay left on Rose River Loop Trail and climb along left bank of river.

[F]   **4.3**   Turn left, uphill, at signpost onto Skyland—Big Meadows Horse Trail [yellow-blazed], which is in old roadbed.

[E]   **4.8**   Reach Rose River Fire Road [yellow-blazed] at Fishers Gap (3061 ft) just below Drive. Turn left onto Rose River Fire Road, descend, pass Dark Hollow Trail [blue-blazed], which enters on right, and cross Hogcamp Branch.

[D]- [A]   **6.2**   Follow directions for *Short Circuit*.

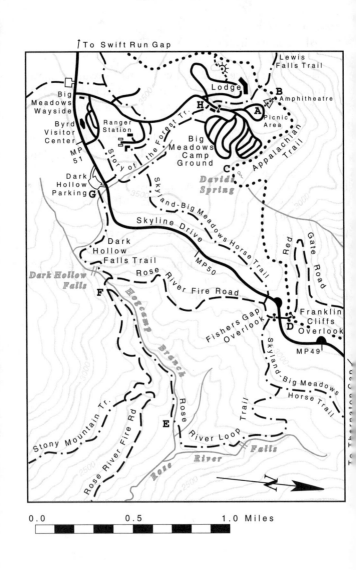

Hike No. 17
DARK HOLLOW

17

	Short Circuit	**Long Circuit**
Length:	3.9 mi	6.4 mi
Time Estimate:	2 hr 30 min	4 hr
Difficulty:	Easy	Moderate
Elev. Change:	900 ft	1400 ft

Description: Both circuits pass Rose River Falls and the site of an old copper mine. Erosion has all but obliterated all traces of this mine. The longer circuit also passes Dark Hollow Falls and offers view points from the Appalachian Trail as it circles the Big Meadows picnic and camping areas. The longer circuit also uses the Story of the Forest Trail, a self-guiding nature trail which passes a botanically interesting wetland. **Dogs are not permitted on the Story of the Forest Trail.**

Access to Short Circuit: Park on west side of Skyline Drive at Fishers Gap, just south of MP 49.

Access to Long Circuit: Drive to Big Meadows, just south of MP 51 on Skyline Drive. Turn in and follow signs to Amphitheater Parking Area.

Directions for Short Circuit:
- **[D]** **0.0** Start at Fishers Gap Parking Area. Cross Drive onto Rose River Fire Road [yellow-blazed]. Continue past horse trail, which enters on left and then exits on right, and descend.
- **[F]** **1.1** Arrive at footbridge over Hogcamp Branch, where Dark Hollow Falls Trail [blue-blazed] enters on right.

CENTRAL DISTRICT

To make side trip to Dark Hollow Falls: Turn right onto Dark Hollow Falls Trail [blue-blazed] and go 0.2 mi to falls.

To continue circuit: Continue on Rose River Fire Road 50 ft past bridge to concrete post at Rose River Loop Trail [blue-blazed]. Turn left onto Rose River Loop Trail and descend along Hogcamp Branch.

[E] **2.1** Turn sharply left and cross Hogcamp Branch. In 250 ft cross small stream and in another 50 ft pass site of old copper mine to left of trail. Approach main branch of Rose River.

3.0 Signpost points right to falls. To continue hike, turn left onto Rose River Loop Trail and climb along left bank of river. Pass Rose River Falls.

3.3 Turn left, uphill, onto Skyland—Big Meadows Horse Trail [yellow-blazed], which is in old roadbed.

[D] **3.9** Turn right onto Rose River Fire Road [yellow-blazed] at Fishers Gap (3061 ft) just below Drive, and continue to Fishers Gap Parking Area.

Directions for Long Circuit:

[A] **0.0** Start at Amphitheater Parking Area, walk to bottom of amphitheater and find *AT* [white-blazed] behind stage. Turn right (north) onto *AT*. A number of unauthorized trails connect to Big Meadows Campground on right. Openings along *AT* give good views north and west. Continue on *AT*.

[C] **0.7** Continue on *AT* past concrete post where *AT* turns sharply to left, away from campground. David Spring is 50 ft to left of trail. Descend through large colony of gray birch. (This is southernmost colony of this northern species.) Cross small stream twice and go through hemlock grove.

1.5 At concrete post, continue on *AT* past spur trail leading 65 yd to Fishers Gap Parking Overlook. (Look for blooming hepatica in spring and clematis in summer.)

[D] **1.6** At Fishers Gap (3061 ft), turn right onto Red Gate Fire Road [yellow-blazed] and cross Drive in 350 ft. Then turn left from fire road onto Skyland—Big Meadows Horse Trail [yellow-blazed] and follow it downhill.

2.2 Turn right onto Rose River Loop Trail [blue-blazed] and descend. Rose River appears on left after a few turns.

2.6 Pass concrete post and continue on Rose River Loop Trail, following Rose River through hemlocks to Rose River Falls (25 ft cascade into deep pool). Turn sharply right, away from falls, but continue downstream.

3.3 Pass concrete post, then turn sharply right. Tailings and ruins of old copper mine are to right of trail just after trail swings away from river (50 ft before trail crosses small stream).

3.4 Cross Hogback Branch on steel bridge and turn sharply right. Stay on Rose River Loop Trail.

[F] **4.4** Turn right at concrete post onto Rose River Fire Road [yellow-blazed] and cross bridge over Hogcamp Branch. Just past bridge, turn left onto Dark Hollow Falls Trail [blue-blazed]. Climb steeply via switchbacks 0.2 mi to Dark Hollow Falls (series of terraced cascades). Continue climbing past falls.

[G] **5.2** Cross Drive before reaching parking area, and in 100 yd Story of the Forest Nature Trail (not blazed) enters on left. Continue ahead (right) on Story of the Forest Nature Trail.

5.5 Pass Skyland—Big Meadows Horse Trail [yellow-blazed] and continue on Story of the Forest Nature Trail.

5.9 At concrete post, turn sharply left to continue on Story of the Forest Nature Trail. Straight ahead is Big Meadows Campground.

[H] **6.0** At paved entrance road to Big Meadows picnic and camping areas, turn right onto paved path to campground registration office. Walk along road to picnic area, keeping left where road forks (wrong way for cars).

[A] **6.4** Arrive back at Amphitheater Parking Area.

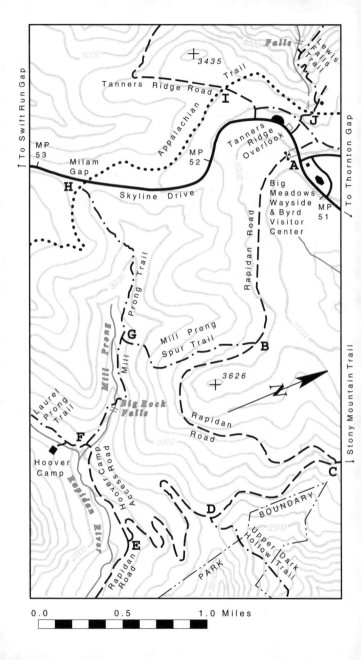

Hike No. 18
HOOVER CAMP

18

Length:	10.2 mi
Time Estimate:	5 hr 45 min
Difficulty:	Moderate
Elev. Change:	1200 ft

Description: Hoover Camp was called the Rapidan River Camp when it was used by President Herbert Hoover and his cabinet as a summer trout fishing camp. In 1929 he held meetings on world armaments with Great Britain's Ramsey McDonald at this camp. Hoover's Lodge, located in a beautiful site at the junction of two streams that form the Rapidan River, has been maintained in excellent condition. In winter this circuit offers fine views from the Rapidan Fire Road, which descends to Hoover Camp. The Camp has informative signs that describe its history. The climb returning from the camp passes a small waterfall and an abandoned orchard in Milam Gap.

Access: Go to Big Meadows Wayside, just south of MP 51 on Skyline Drive.

Directions:
[A] 0.0 Start at Big Meadows Wayside and cross Drive to Rapidan Fire Road, which is diagonally across from entrance to Big Meadows. Go past gate and concrete post and hike along road through meadows and into forest.
[B] 1.3 Pass Mill Prong Spur Trail [yellow-blazed], which enters on right, and continue on Rapidan Fire Road. (Mill Prong Spur Trail leads 1.8 mi down to Hoover Camp and can be used as shortcut.) Road descends via switchbacks into Rapidan River Valley. Occasionally Fork Mtn,

Doubletop Mtn, Old Rag Mtn, and Rapidan River Valley can be seen.

[C] **3.0** Stony Mtn Trail [yellow-blazed] enters on left. Continue on road.

[D] **3.9** Upper Dark Hollow Trail [yellow-blazed] enters on left. Continue to descend on road to Camp Hoover access road.

[E] **5.7** Turn right onto access road and climb.

[F] **6.2** Hoover Camp is 250 ft ahead on access road. To complete circuit, cross bridge and go 100 ft. Turn right onto Mill Prong Trail [blue-blazed] and follow it along Mill Prong.

6.6 Cross to right side of Mill Prong just below Big Rock Falls. This crossing is easy to miss.

[G] **7.1** Continue straight on Mill Prong Trail, which goes straight ahead as Mill Prong Spur Trail turns right. Bear left, ford small branch of Mill Prong, and then climb through tall trees and carpet of ferns toward Milam Gap.

7.5 Cross main branch of Mill Prong and climb through overgrown fields and abandoned orchard.

[H] **8.1** Turn right (north) at concrete post onto *AT* [white-blazed] at Milam Gap, cross Drive, go through field, and enter woods.

8.9 Pass spring 50 ft to right of trail.

[I] **9.2** Cross Tanners Ridge Road and continue past cemetery. Pass housed-in Lewis Spring.

[J] **9.8** Turn right onto service road and climb, then turn left onto Drive.

[A] **10.2** Arrive back at Big Meadows Wayside.

Hike No. 19
LEWIS SPRING FALLS

19

Length:	3.3 mi
Time Estimate:	2 hr
Difficulty:	Easy
Elev. Change:	1200 ft

Description: Lewis Spring Falls is reached via an interesting trail which winds down a rocky hillside. The return trail passes by rocks that provide a grandstand view westward to the Shenandoah Valley, Massanutten Mountain, Great North Mountain, and the distant Appalachians.

Access: Go to Big Meadows Wayside, on west side of Skyline Drive just south of MP 51. Three parking areas are available: one is large lot at Big Meadows Wayside and Visitors Center; one is on east side of Drive 100 yd north of service road where circuit begins; and one is 20 yd south of service road on east side of Drive.

Directions:
- **[A] 0.0** Find gated service road just south of Big Meadows Wayside on west side of Drive. Turn right onto service road and descend past horse trail to *AT* [white-blazed].
- **[B] 0.2** Cross *AT* and continue downhill short distance to Lewis Spring Falls Trail [blue-blazed]. Turn left onto Lewis Spring Falls Trail and continue to concrete post at spur trail junction.
- **[C] 0.8** Turn left onto spur trail to top of Lewis Spring Falls in 150 ft.

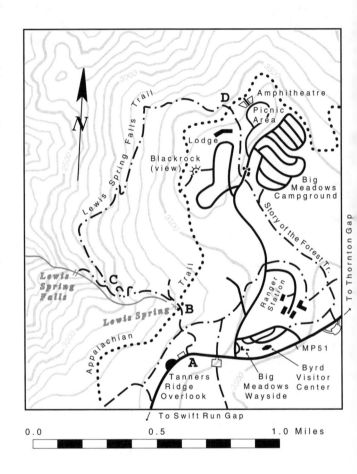

N

3000

2500

3500

Lewis Spring Falls Trail

Amphitheatre

D

Picnic Area

Lodge

Blackrock (view)

3500

Big Meadows Campground

Story of the Forest Tr.

Lewis Spring Falls

C

Lewis Spring Falls Trail

Ranger Station

Lewis Spring

B

3000

Appalachian

3000

A

Tanners Ridge Overlook

Big Meadows Wayside

MP51

Byrd Visitor Center

3500

To Thornton Gap

To Swift Run Gap

0.0   0.5   1.0 Miles

CENTRAL DISTRICT

To get to base of falls: Follow trail behind and to right of warning sign at top of falls and descend cliff via steep, rocky switchbacks. Bottom of falls is 0.2 mi from top.

To continue circuit: Climb back up spur trail to concrete post, turn left onto Lewis Spring Falls Trail, and descend steeply. Continue on Lewis Spring Falls Trail to concrete post at *AT*.

[D] **2.0** Turn right (south) onto *AT*.

2.3 To left are sheer cliffs of Blackrock. Rock outcrops to right of trail provide grandstand views westward. Continue to concrete post at spur trail that enters on right. (Spur trail leads 0.1 mi to viewpoint on Blackrock, and another 0.2 mi to Big Meadows Lodge.)

2.4 Stay on *AT* and hike along western slope of ridge to service road, with occasional views to west from rocks to right of trail.

[B] **3.0** Turn left onto service road.

[A] **3.3** Arrive back at parking areas on Drive.

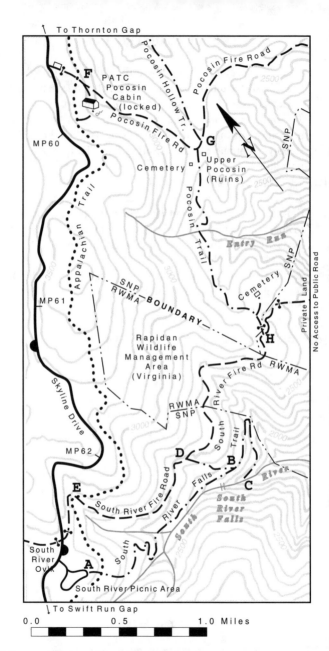

To Thornton Gap

Pocosin Hollow Tr.

Pocosin Fire Road

2500

F
PATC
Pocosin Cabin
(locked)

Pocosin Fire Rd

MP 60

G

Cemetery

Upper Pocosin (Ruins)

Appalachian Trail

2500

SNP

Entry Run

MP 61

SNP
RWMA
BOUNDARY

3000

Cemetery

Skyline Drive

H

Private Land

No Access to Public Road

SNP

Rapidan Wildlife Management Area (Virginia)

RWMA

River

RWMA
SNP

3000

South River Fire Rd

2500

MP 62

D

South River Trail

B

2000

C

E

South River Fire Road

River Falls

South River Falls

South River Ovlk

South River

A

2500

South River Picnic Area

To Swift Run Gap

0.0   0.5   1.0 Miles

Hike No. 20
SOUTH RIVER FALLS

20

	Short Circuit	**Long Circuit**
Length:	4.4 mi	10.0 mi
Time Estimate:	2 hr 45 min	5 hr 45 min
Difficulty:	Easy	Moderate
Elev. Change:	800 ft	1800 ft

Description: Both circuits go to South River Falls and use the South River Falls Trail. This graded trail leads down into the deep, wooded gorge of South River to South River Falls, a 70-foot waterfall that consists of an upper and lower cascade. The *Long Circuit* passes Kites Deadening and Pocosin Cabin. Kites Deadening was once the site of farm fields. Rather than felling trees to clear a field, early settlers girdled the trees, removed the lower bark (thus killing the trees), and then planted their crops among the "deadened" trees—thus "Kites Deadening." "Pocosin" is said to be a Native American word meaning "dismal" or "swamp." The cabin is a locked structure available for use through advance reservation with the PATC. This circuit also passes two old cemeteries and the ruins of Upper Pocosin Mission.

Access: Go to South River Picnic Area on Skyline Drive just north of MP 63.

Directions for Short Circuit:
[A] **0.0** Go to eastern-most point of road through South River Picnic Area, find sign for South River Falls Trail [blue-blazed], and begin hike.

  0.1 Cross *AT* [white-blazed] and continue downhill on South River Falls Trail.

1.0 Reach viewpoint at top of falls. Do not take any spur trails at top of falls. (Park Service has attempted to block all trails that lead to edge of falls because this area is dangerous.) Continue descending.

[B] **1.2** Keep right past old road which enters on left and continue on South River Falls Trail.

[C] **1.8** At South River, turn right onto rough foot trail which leads 450 ft to base of falls.

1.9 To continue circuit, retrace steps back to old road.

[B] **2.6** Turn right onto old road.

[D] **3.0** Turn left onto South River Fire Road [yellow-blazed] and climb.

[E] **3.8** Turn left (south) onto *AT*.

4.3 Turn right onto South River Falls Trail [blue-blazed] at four-way intersection.

[A] **4.4** Arrive back at South River Falls Picnic Area.

Long Circuit Directions:

[A] **0.0** Go to eastern-most point of road through South River Picnic Area, find sign for South River Falls Trail [blue-blazed], and begin hike.

0.1 Turn left (north) onto *AT* [white-blazed].

[E] **0.6** Cross South River Fire Road [yellow-blazed]. Begin long, gentle ascent of Baldface Mtn.

1.5 Cross old road. (To right, road leads past old quarry.)

1.9 Rocks to right of trail offer views westward.

2.2 Reach summit of Baldface Mtn (3600 ft) and begin gentle descent.

3.0 Pass through relatively flat area known as Kites Deadening.

3.1 Reach view north to Lewis Mtn, Hazeltop, Jones Mtn, and Fork Mtn (with radio tower), then descend steeply via switchbacks.

3.3 Pass spring to left of trail.

3.4 Continue past spur trail that leads right, downhill, 250 ft to Pocosin Cabin and spring to south of cabin. (Three mountains are visible from cabin—from right to left: Panther, Bear Stand, and Sawney Macks; these names are not shown on modern maps.) Pass spur trail and descend gently on *AT*.

[F] **3.5** Turn right onto Pocosin Fire Road [yellow-blazed].

3.6 Pass Pocosin Cabin, which is on right side of road, and descend into gap.

[G] **4.5** Turn right at signpost onto Pocosin Trail [yellow-blazed]. A few ft past this turn, ruins of Upper Pocosin Mission are to left of trail and small cemetery with field-stone headstones is barely visible on right.

5.7 Pass through abandoned apple orchard to flat, grassy area and turn right onto Pocosin Trail. (Spur trail leads 0.1 mi straight ahead to interesting South River cemetery, which is covered by periwinkles in summer.)

[H] **5.8** Turn right onto South River Fire Road [yellow-blazed].

[D] **7.0** Turn left, downhill, at signpost onto old road.

[B] **7.4** Turn left onto South River Falls Trail [blue-blazed].

[C] **8.0** At South River, turn right onto rough foot trail which leads 450 ft to base of falls.

8.1 To continue circuit, retrace steps back to South River Falls Trail.

[B] **8.8** Stay left to continue on South River Falls Trail. Old road enters from right.

9.0 Reach viewpoint at head of falls. Continue on South River Falls Trail. Do not take any spur trails at top of falls. (Park Service has attempted to block all trails that lead to edge of falls because this area is dangerous.)

9.9 Cross *AT* and continue uphill.

[A] **10.0** Arrive back at South River Falls Picnic Area.

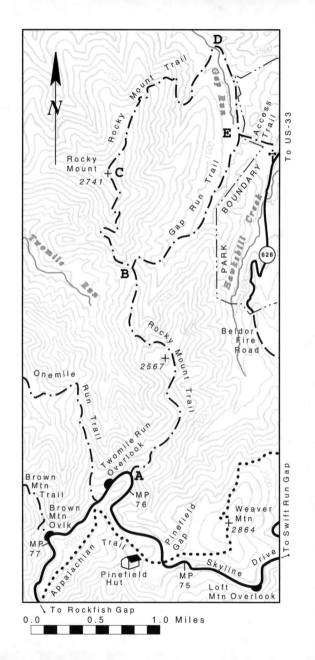

N

Rocky Mount Trail

Gap Run

D

1500

To US-33

E

Access Trail

Rocky Mount
2741

+C

PARK BOUNDARY

Gap Run Trail

628

Twomile Run

B

Rocky Mount Trail

+2567

Onemile Run Trail

Beldor Fire Road

Twomile Run Overlook

A

MP 76

Brown Mtn Trail

Brown Mtn Ovlk

MP 77

Appalachian Trail

Pinefield Gap

Pinefield Hut

Weaver Mtn
+2864

To Swift Run Gap

Skyline Drive

MP 75

Loft Mtn Overlook

To Rockfish Gap

0.0   0.5   1.0 Miles

Hike No. 21
ROCKY MOUNT

21

Length:	9.8 mi
Time Estimate:	6 hr 15 min
Difficulty:	Strenuous
Elev. Change:	2600 ft

Description: This circuit traverses a wild, rugged area. The Rocky Mount Trail leads along a side ridge that runs north to the peak of Rocky Mount (2741 ft) with a spectacular view across Twomile Run Valley. Then the trail descends steeply 400 ft on a rough, rocky trail to Gap Run.

Access: Trail begins at sharp curve in Skyline Drive just south of MP 76 and just north of Twomile Run Overlook. Park at Overlook.

Directions:
- **[A] 0.0** From Twomile Run Overlook, walk north along Drive to trailhead. Start hike at concrete post at Rocky Mount Trail [blue-blazed]. Follow ridge northward with many fine views.
- **[B] 2.2** In sag continue on Rocky Mount Trail past Gap Run Trail [blue-blazed], which intersects from right. (Return route comes to this point.) Climb past views of Twomile Run Valley to summit of Rocky Mount.
- **[C] 3.4** Cliffs beyond summit offer fine views. Descend steeply from summit toward Twomile Run Valley.
  - **4.6** Turn right sharply as trail becomes rocky.
  - **4.9** Cross small stream twice.
- **[D] 5.4** Ford Gap Run, then turn right at concrete post onto Gap Run Trail [blue-blazed].
  - **5.9** Follow blue blazes left around obstruction.
- **[E] 6.2** Keep right on Gap Run Trail where old road enters straight ahead.
- **[B] 7.6** Turn left at concrete post onto Rocky Mount Trail.
- **[A] 9.8** Arrive back at trailhead on Drive. Walk south along Drive to Twomile Run Overlook.

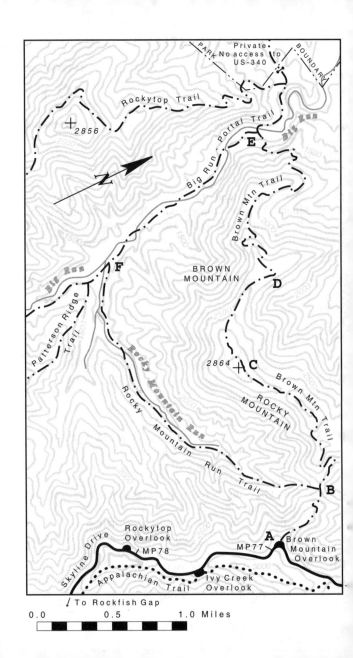

PARK BOUNDARY

Private No access to US-340

BOUNDARY

Rockytop Trail

+ 2856

2500

Big Run Portal Trail

E

Big Run

1500

Big Run

Brown Mtn Trail

2000

BROWN
MOUNTAIN

1500

Big Run

F

1500

Patterson Ridge Trail

D

Rocky Mountain Run

2864 + C

Brown Mtn Trail

Rocky Mountain Run Trail

ROCKY
MOUNTAIN

2500

2000

B

Skyline Drive

Rockytop Overlook
MP78

A MP77

Brown Mountain Overlook

Appalachian Trail

Ivy Creek Overlook

3000

To Rockfish Gap

0.0   0.5   1.0 Miles

Hike No. 22
ROCKY MTN— BROWN MTN

22

Length:	9.8 mi
Time Estimate:	6 hr
Difficulty:	**Strenuous—recommended for experienced hikers only**
Elev. Change:	2100 ft

Description: The South District of SNP has a Rocky Mount, a Rocky Mountain, and a Rockytop. The people who named these mountains were obviously impressed with the rugged cliffs, rock slides, and rocky streams in this area. This circuit takes the hiker on a graded trail along the crest of the Rocky Mountain—Brown Mountain ridge, to the summits of Rocky Mountain (2864 ft) and Brown Mountain (2560 ft), and then down into Big Run Valley. The ridge runs east-west and offers extraordinary views: to the north is the lower Twomile Ridge, with Rocky Mount in the background; to the south is the high, imposing ridge that leads to Rockytop. Between the crest of Rocky Mountain and Brown Mountain, the trail passes through an area damaged by fire in 1986. This area supports a profusion of turkeybeard, a grass-like member of the lily family that blooms spectacularly in late May-early June. The trail also passes many stands of mountain laurel, which bloom at the same time. The ridge on Brown Mountain is composed of sandstone streaked with 500 million year-old fossil worm holes, which appear as long, slender cylindrical markings about an eighth of an inch in diameter. This circuit fords Big Run and Rocky Mountain Run several times. These fords become wades when the water is high. The fire damage and subsequent gypsy moth damage on Rocky Mount have destroyed most of the large trees, so there is very little shade on this portion of the circuit. Be sure to carry extra water in summer months.

SOUTH DISTRICT

Access: Go to Brown Mtn Overlook on Skyline Drive just north of MP 77 and park.

Directions:
- **[A] 0.0**   Go through opening in retaining wall at Brown Mtn Overlook (marked by signpost) and descend on Brown Mtn Trail [blue-blazed].
- **[B] 0.7**   Reach concrete post at gap where Rocky Mtn Run Trail [blue-blazed] enters on left. (Return route comes to this point.) Continue straight on Brown Mtn Trail.
- **[C] 1.6**   Reach highest point of circuit at crest of Rocky Mtn, with spectacular views west to Massanutten Mtn. Beyond this point, footing becomes rugged as trail descends slightly and then climbs toward second peak.

  2.2   Pass to right of second, highest peak of Rocky Mtn. Fossil worm holes are visible in outcrops here. Short bushwacks to rock outcrops are rewarded by extraordinary views. Descend slightly and then climb.
- **[D] 3.1**   Descend from summit of Brown Mtn along ridge crest that offers spectacular views of Shenandoah Valley, Rockytop, and southern end of Massanutten Mtn. Outcrops on left of trail show fossil worm holes. Turn off ridge line and descend steeply.
- **[E] 5.3**   Reach Big Run and turn left onto Big Run—Portal Trail [yellow-blazed]. (To right 0.5 mi is "The Portal," a narrow gorge with impressive cliffs and talus slopes.) Continue up-stream on trail and ford Big Run twice.

  6.3   To left of trail is flat, brushy area that was once field. Evidence of old homestead can be seen. Continue on trail, ford run twice more.
- **[F] 6.7**   At fork, turn left onto Rocky Mtn Run Trail [blue-blazed] and climb steeply along Rocky Mtn Run, fording run several times.
- **[B] 9.4**   Turn right, uphill, at concrete post onto Brown Mtn Trail.
- **[A] 10.1**   Arrive back at Brown Mtn Overlook.

Hike No. 23
BIG RUN LOOP TRAIL

23

	Short Circuit	**Long Circuit**
Length:	6.0 mi	7.0 mi
Time Estimate:	3 hr 45 min	4 hr 15 min
Difficulty:	Moderate	Moderate
Elev. Change:	1400 ft	1600 ft

Description: Both circuits descend 1140 ft from Big Run Overlook on Skyline Drive to the upper end of Big Run Valley, then climb onto the ridge that defines the Big Run watershed. Here they join the Appalachian Trail and parallel Skyline Drive back to the Overlook. The *Long Circuit* reaches Browns Gap, which General Stonewall Jackson used to move troops several times during the Civil War's Valley Campaign.

Access: Both circuits begin at Big Run Overlook, just south of MP 81 on Skyline Drive. Parking areas at Big Run Overlook are usually full on summer weekends. Alternate parking is at Doyles River Parking Area, just north of MP 82. (If you park at Doyles River Parking Area, follow *AT* [white-blazed] north to Doyles River Trail [blue-blazed] to get to point [A].)

Directions for Short Circuit:

[A] **0.0** From Big Run Overlook, descend steeply via switch-backs on Big Run Loop Trail [blue-blazed here].

0.7 Follow crest of ridge between branches of Big Run. Then swing left, down into main hollow.

[B] **2.2** Cross branch of Big Run. At Big Run—Portal Trail [yellow-blazed], turn left to stay on Big Run Loop Trail. (This section of trail is dual-blazed blue and yellow.) Climb

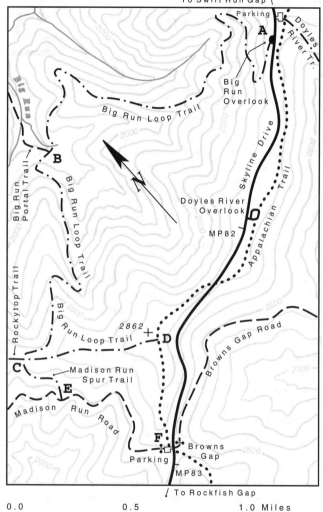

To Swift Run Gap

Parking

A

Doyles River Tr.

Big Run Overlook

Big Run Loop Trail

Big Run

B

Big Run Portal Trail

Big Run Loop Trail

Skyline Drive

Doyles River Overlook

MP 82

Appalachian Trail

Rockytop Trail

Big Run Loop Trail

2862

D

C

Madison Run Spur Trail

Browns Gap Road

E

Madison Run Road

F

Browns Gap

Parking

MP 83

To Rockfish Gap

0.0   0.5   1.0 Miles

steadily through standing dead trees along ravine above branch of Big Run.

     3.0   Turn sharply right, away from ravine and ascend.

[C] **3.5**   Turn left, uphill, at concrete post at four-way intersection with Rockytop Trail [blue-blazed] and continue on Big Run Loop Trail [blue-blazed here].

[D] **4.2**   Turn left (north) onto *AT* [white-blazed].

     4.5   Cross Drive and continue on *AT*. Crossing offers fine view of Cedar Mtn and Trayfoot Mtn.

     4.7   Follow ledge that offers views in winter.

     4.9   Pass through Doyles River Parking Overlook and continue on *AT*.

     5.9   Turn left, uphill, onto Doyles River Trail [blue-blazed] and in a few ft cross Drive.

[A] **6.0**   Arrive back at Big Run Overlook.

Directions for Long Circuit:

[A] - [B] Follow directions for *Short Circuit*.

[C] **3.5**   Continue straight across gap onto Madison Run Spur Trail and descend.

[E] **3.8**   Turn left onto Madison Run Fire Road [yellow-blazed].

[F] **4.6**   Reach Drive at Browns Gap (2599 ft). Turn left (north) onto *AT* [white-blazed] at concrete post—do not cross Drive. Ascend 250 ft and then level off.

[D] - [A] **5.2**   Pass Big Run Loop Trail and continue on *AT* to Drive. Follow directions for *Short Circuit* from crossing Drive (*Short Circuit* mileage 4.5) to Big Run Overlook.

To Swift Run Gap, US-33

MP 81

Parking

A

PATC
Doyles River
Cabin (locked)

Doyles

Big Run Loop Trail

G

River Trail

Big Run Overlook

2500

Appalachian Trail

F

Browns Gap Road

Doyles River Overlook

B

2500

Falls

MP 82

Doyles River Trail

C

2000

Browns Gap Road

2862

D

Falls

N

Big Run Loop Trail

2500

Madison Run Rd.

E

Browns Gap

Parking

MP 83

To Rockfish Gap, US-250

0.0   0.5   1.0 Miles

Hike No. 24
THE SOURCE

24

Length:	5.0 mi
Time Estimate:	2 hr 45 min
Difficulty:	Moderate
Elev. Change:	700 ft

Description: This circuit goes through Browns Gap (Browns Gap Fire Road) which General Stonewall Jackson's troops used during the Civil War's Valley Campaign to make raids into Shenandoah Valley. Then the circuit passes the grave of William H. Howard, Company F, 44th Virginia Infantry, CSA. Whether Howard died of injuries or disease is unknown. This circuit also includes a section of the Doyles River Trail, which was constructed by the CCC in 1936-37.

Access: Go to Doyles River Cabin Parking Area (2800 ft) on east side of Skyline Drive 0.1 mi south of MP 81.

Directions:
- **[A] 0.0** Find Doyles River Trail [blue-blazed] and go 200 ft to *AT* [white-blazed]. Turn right (south) onto *AT*. Trail closely parallels Drive and is fairly level.
- **[B] 1.0** Continue through Doyles River Overlook Parking Area and follow ledges that offer excellent views south in winter.
- **[C] 1.4** Cross Drive. Cedar and Trayfoot Mtns are visible from Drive.
- **[D] 1.7** Pass Big Run Loop Trail [blue-blazed], which enters on right. Continue on *AT* and descend gradually.
- **[E] 2.3** Pass concrete post marking Madison Run Fire Road [yellow-blazed] at Browns Gap Parking Area (2599 ft).

Continue on *AT* through Parking Area and in 100 ft cross Drive diagonally.

2.4 Turn left onto Browns Gap Fire Road [yellow-blazed] and descend gently.

2.8 To left short, steep footpath leads to concrete post at William H. Howard's grave. Continue on fire road, pass ancient tulip poplar of tremendous girth, and cross metal footbridge.

[F] **4.0** Turn left onto Doyles River Trail [blue-blazed] and ascend. Pass spur trail and spring on right. (Spur trail leads steeply uphill 0.1 mi to Doyles River Cabin, PATC cabin for use by advance reservation only.)

4.9 Cross *AT*.

[A] **5.0** Arrive at Doyles River Cabin Parking Area.

Hike No. 25
ROCKYTOP

25

Length:	12.9 mi
Time Estimate:	7 hr 45 min
Difficulty:	**Strenuous—recommended for experienced hikers only**
Elev. Change:	2440 ft

Description: This circuit traverses rugged scenery composed of Rockytop's high ridges and deep stream valleys and fords Big Run several times. The trails offer spectacular southward views of peaks and the Shenandoah Valley in winter, but summer foliage blocks these views except in the most exposed rocky areas. Rockytop Trail extends across the crest of Rockytop, which forms the sheer southwest wall of Big Run Canyon. Fossilized worm holes are in some of the rock where the trail crosses rock slides or talus slopes. The worm holes appear as long, slender cylindrical markings with a diameter of about an eighth of an inch. The trail passes many stands of turkeybeard, a grass-like member of the lily family that blooms spectacularly in mid May-early June. This circuit fords Big Run seven times and fords side streams twice. These fords become wades when the water is high.

Access: Go to Browns Gap Parking Area (2599 ft) on west side of Skyline Drive, 0.1 mi north of MP 83. (General Stonewall Jackson's troops used Browns Gap during Civil War's Valley Campaign to make raids into Shenandoah Valley.)

Directions:
[A] 0.0 Find *AT* [white-blazed] at concrete post at north edge of parking area and climb.

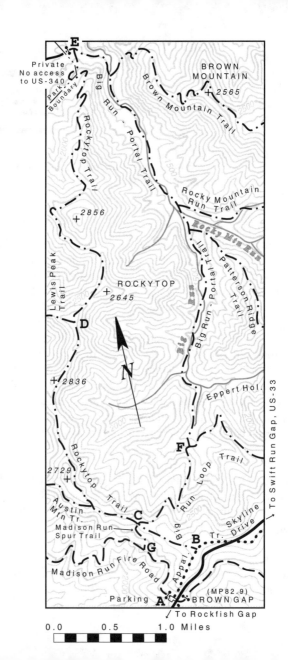

E

BROWN MOUNTAIN

Private
No access
to US-340

+2565

Park Boundary

Brown Mountain Trail

Rockytop Trail

Big Run - Portal Trail

Rocky Mountain Run Trail

Rocky Mtn Run

+2856

Lewis Peak Trail

ROCKYTOP
+2645

Big Run

Big Run - Portal Trail

Patterson Ridge Trail

D

N

+2836

Eppert Hol.

F

To Swift Run Gap, US-33

Rockytop Trail

Big Run Loop Trail

2729
+

Austin Mtn Tr.

C

Skyline Drive

Madison Run
Spur Trail

G

B Tr. Dr.

To Rockfish Gap

Appal. Tr.

Madison Run Fire Road

(MP 82.9)

Parking **A** BROWN GAP

To Rockfish Gap

0.0   0.5   1.0 Miles

SOUTH DISTRICT

[B] **0.5** Turn left onto Big Run Loop Trail [blue-blazed].

[C] **1.2** Reach concrete post at junction with Rockytop Trail [blue-blazed] and Madison Run Spur Trail [yellow-blazed] in hollow. (Return route comes to this intersection.) Continue straight ahead, across hollow, onto Rockytop Trail and ascend.

1.6 At fork, go right to continue on Rockytop Trail where Austin Mtn Trail [blue-blazed] enters on left. Skirt right side of ridge, then swing to left side and cross talus slope that offers views of Austin and Lewis Mtns.

[D] **3.5** Turn right at intersection with Lewis Peak Trail [blue-blazed] and continue on Rockytop Trail.

4.3 Reach hollow at base of Rockytop's highest peak (2856 ft) and ascend along its western slope.

4.8 Cross talus slope with outstanding views of Austin Mtn, Lewis Mtn, and Lewis Peak to southwest, and Shenandoah Valley and Massanutten Mtn to north. Many rocks here and on rocky slopes beyond are so full of fossilized worm holes that they have striated appearance.

5.0 Bear right, ascend by switchbacks over crest of ridge, and then descend. (Hangman Run splits main ridge here.)

6.7 Cross Park Boundary and exit Park. Reenter Park within 0.1 mi.

[E] **7.0** Turn right at concrete post onto Big Run—Portal Trail [yellow-blazed]. (To left, one can bushwack down to Big Run at "The Portal," a narrow gorge with impressive cliffs and talus slopes.) Continue upstream on Big Run—Portal Trail.

7.4 Cross bridge to east bank of Big Run. Pass concrete post and continue on Big Run—Portal Trail where Brown Mtn Trail [blue-blazed] enters on left.

7.8 Ford Big Run to west bank, then ford Big Run again in 0.4 mi, again in another 0.4 mi, and once more in another 0.2 mi.

8.9 Take right fork to stay on Big Run—Portal Trail where Rocky Mtn Run Trail [blue-blazed] enters on left.

9.0 Ford Rocky Mtn Run and continue on Big Run's east bank.

9.1 Pass concrete post and continue on Big Run—Portal Trail where Patterson Ridge Trail [yellow-blazed] enters from left.

9.9 Ford Big Run to west bank, cross again in 0.3 mi, and again in another 0.1 mi.

10.6 Ford two small side creeks (last fords).

[F] **11.3** Turn right at concrete signpost onto Big Run Loop Trail [dual-blazed blue and yellow] and climb.

[C] **12.6** At concrete post on ridge, turn left to continue on Big Run Loop Trail [blue-blazed here].

[B] **13.2** Turn right (south) onto *AT* at concrete post and descend.

[A] **13.8** Arrive at Browns Gap Parking Area on Drive.

Hike No. 26
DOYLES RIVER TRAIL

26

	Short Circuit	**Long Circuit**
Length:	6.6 mi	8.4 mi
Time Estimate:	4 hr	5 hr
Difficulty:	Moderate	Moderate
Elev. Change:	1400 ft	1800 ft

Description: These circuits offer rewarding hikes along the east slope of the Blue Ridge. Originally constructed by the CCC in 1936-37, they feature waterfalls along Doyles River and Jones Run. Doyles River and Jones Run are located in deep gorges with broken, precipitous cliffs and enormous trees. Both circuits descend 1330 ft past waterfalls on Jones Run to Doyles River, and then climb back up the steep and narrow trail along Doyles River, past two more waterfalls. The lower falls drop 63 ft in a two-step cascade between high rock cliffs. The upper falls are a three-step cascade in a picturesque canyon. Both circuits go to Browns Gap, which General Stonewall Jackson's troops used during the Civil War's Valley Campaign to make raids into Shenandoah Valley. The short circuit follows part of Jackson's route through the gap and passes the grave of William H. Howard, Company F, 44th Virginia Infantry, CSA. Whether Howard died of injuries or disease is unknown.

Access: Both circuits begin at Jones Run Parking Area (2700 ft), just south of MP 84 on Skyline Drive.

Directions for Short Circuit:
[A] **0.0** Descend eastward from Jones Run Parking Area on Jones Run Trail [blue-blazed]. Cross *AT* [white-blazed] in 100 ft and continue descending.

To Thornton Gap

MP 81

Parking

E

PATC
Doyles River
Cabin (locked)

D

Doyles

River Trail

Falls

C

Browns Gap Road

Big Run Loop Tr.

Appalachian

Trail

Doyles River
Overlook

MP 82

Falls

Doyles River

2500

B

Browns

Gap

Road

2862 +

Big Run
Loop Trail

Madison Run Road

BROWNS GAP

Parking

K

F

MP 83

Falls

Jones Run

DUNDO HOLLOW

Skyline Drive

Dundo Group Camp-
ground

Jones Run Trail

Dundo Overlook

MP 84

Parking

A

To Rockfish Gap

0.0   0.5   1.0 Miles

0.6 Cross Jones Run.

1.5 Return to Jones Run and follow south bank.

1.6 Jones Run forms sloping waterfall.

1.7 Pass top of 42 ft waterfall. Short spur trail provides good view of falls.

2.0 Pass top of lower falls.

[B] 2.5 Just before junction of Jones Run and Doyles River, trail swings left. Jones Run Trail turns into Doyles River Trail here. This area supports a wide variety of wildflowers such as bloodroot, Dutchman's breeches, cutleaf toothwort, and hepatica. Continue circuit on Doyles River Trail [blue-blazed] and climb along Doyles River.

3.2 Reach top of lower falls.

3.5 Reach top of upper falls.

[C] 3.8 Turn left onto Browns Gap Fire Road [yellow-blazed] and climb easy grade past ancient tulip poplar of enormous girth.

5.1 To right, short footpath leads to concrete post at William H. Howard's grave.

[F] 5.4 Turn left (south) onto *AT* at Browns Gap Parking Area (do not cross Drive) and climb gently.

6.1 Skirt eastern side of Dundo developed area for 0.2 mi. Several spur trails lead up to Dundo, where water can be obtained from May to October. Turn sharply left where spur trail leads right to Dundo. Continue on *AT*.

[A] 6.6 Arrive back at Jones Run Parking Area.

Directions for Long Circuit:

[A] - [B] Follow directions for *Short Circuit.*

[C] 3.8 Pass Browns Gap Fire Road [yellow-blazed] and continue climbing on Doyles River Trail.

[D] 4.4 Pass spring on right of trail. (Spur trail leads right 0.1 mi steeply uphill to Doyles River Cabin, PATC cabin for use by advance reservation only.)

[E] 4.7 Turn left (south) onto *AT*. Trail closely parallels Drive and is fairly level.

5.6 Follow *AT* through Doyles River Overlook.

5.8 Follow ledges which offer views south in winter.

6.0 Cross Drive. Cedar Mtn and Trayfoot Mtn are visible.

6.3 Stay on *AT* where Big Run Loop Trail [blue-blazed] enters on right and begin gradual descent.

[F] 6.9 Pass concrete post at Madison Fire Road [yellow-blazed] in Browns Gap (2599 ft) and continue on *AT*. In 100 ft cross Drive diagonally.

7.0 Go through Browns Gap Parking Area and continue past Browns Gap Fire Road, which enters on left.

7.7 Skirt eastern side of Dundo developed area for 0.2 mi. Several spur trails lead up to Dundo, where water can be obtained from May to October.

7.8 Turn sharply left where spur trail leads right to Dundo. Continue on *AT*.

[A] 8.4 Arrive back at Jones Run Parking Area.

Hike No. 27
AUSTIN MTN—
FURNACE MTN

27

Length:	12.6 mi
Time Estimate:	7 hr 45 min
Difficulty:	**Strenuous—recommended for experienced hikers only**
Elev. Change:	2500 ft

Description: This is a difficult hike that ranges across the western slopes of Austin Mountain toward outlying, conical peaks of the Blue Ridge. The circuit can include a 0.5 mi side trip to the summit of Furnace Mountain (2657 ft), which offers excellent views. Furnace Mountain lies within a wilderness area and is in one of the most remote sections of the Park. The circuit can also include a 0.1 mi side trip to Blackrock (3092 ft), a tumbled mass of lichen-covered stone that offers spectacular views. Sections of this circuit are rocky, steep, and poorly graded. Heavy-duty foot gear is recommended. This circuit can be hiked from either the Park's western boundary or from Skyline Drive. Directions are provided from the Park Boundary.

Access from Park Boundary: Take US 340 to Grottoes, Va and turn east onto SR 663. Follow SR 663 past SR 659, SR 708, and unnumbered road that enters on left (2.8 mi). Park at unnumbered road. SR 663 turns into Madison Run Fire Road, which continues ahead 0.2 mi to chained gate at Park Boundary (1360 ft). **Fire road is not wide enough to turn around or park, so do not drive beyond suggested parking area.**

Access from Skyline Drive: Go to Browns Gap Parking Area, 0.1 mi north of MP 83. Begin circuit at [G].

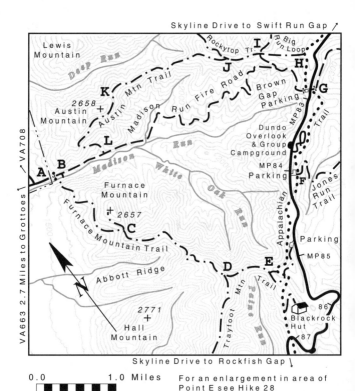

Skyline Drive to Swift Run Gap ↗

Lewis
Mountain

Deep Run

Rockytop Tr

Big
Run Loop

I

H

J

Brown
Gap
Parking

G

Austin Mtn Trail

Madison Run Fire Road

MP83

K

2658
Austin
Mountain

Dundo
Overlook
& Group
Campground

Trail

L

MP84
Parking

Run

Appalachian

A B

White

Oak

F

Jones
Run
Trail

Madison

Run

Furnace
Mountain

Furnace Mountain Trail

2657

C

Run

Parking
MP85

VA663 2.7 Miles to Grottoes

VA708

Abbott Ridge

D

E

N

Trayfoot Mtn Trail

Paine Run

86

Blackrock
Hut

2771
Hall
Mountain

87

Skyline Drive to Rockfish Gap ↓

0.0   1.0 Miles

For an enlargement in area of
Point E see Hike 28

For an enlargement in area of
Points G to J see Hike 25

SOUTH DISTRICT

Directions:

[A] **0.0** From unnumbered road, hike up Madison Run Fire Road [yellow-blazed].

0.2 Pass chain at Park Boundary and continue on fire road.

[B] **0.3** Turn right at concrete post onto Furnace Mtn Trail [blue-blazed]. (Return route comes to this point.) Cross Madison Run and follow it back downstream for about 100 ft before beginning to climb Furnace Mtn. (In summer, trail along run may be obscured by new growth.)

[C] **1.9** Spur trail [blue-blazed] enters on left.

To go to peak of Furnace Mtn: Turn left onto spur trail and hike 0.5 mi to ledge with excellent view of Madison Run Valley and Austin Mtn.

To continue circuit: Continue uphill on Furnace Mtn Trail from junction with spur trail.

3.0 Turn sharply left to stay on Furnace Mtn Trail.

[D] **3.7** Turn left onto Trayfoot Mtn Trail [blue-blazed].

[E] **4.2** At ridge crest, Blackrock Spur Trail [blue-blazed] enters on left. (Blackrock Spur Trail is narrower than Trayfoot Mtn Trail.) Turn left onto Blackrock Spur Trail.

4.3 Turn left (north) onto *AT* [white-blazed]. (To right *AT* goes to Blackrock in 0.1 mi.)

4.5 *AT* and Trayfoot Mtn Trail come within a few ft of one another and run parallel for about 0.1 mi, but do not cross.

4.6 At concrete post, *AT* is briefly concurrent with blue-blazed Trayfoot Mtn Trail, which leads right 750 ft to Drive and parking lot. Continue on *AT*.

5.4 Cross to right side of Drive and pass through remains of abandoned apple orchard.

[F] **5.6** Pass Jones Run Trail [blue-blazed] (parking lot is 50 ft to left). Continue on *AT* along fairly level terrain.

6.1 Turn sharply to right where spur trail leads straight ahead to Dundo developed area. (Water is available at

Dundo from May to October.) Continue on *AT*. Beyond Dundo, descend gradually.

[G] 6.8 Cross Drive and continue on *AT* past concrete post marking Madison Run Fire Road [yellow-blazed] on north side of Browns Gap Parking Area (2599 ft). Ascend 250 ft and then level off.

[H] 7.4 Turn left at concrete post onto Big Run Loop Trail [blue-blazed].

[I] 8.1 Concrete post in hollow marks junction with Rockytop Trail [blue-blazed] and Madison Run Spur Trail [yellow-blazed]. Continue straight ahead onto Rockytop Trail and ascend.

[J] 8.5 At fork, turn left onto Austin Mtn Trail [blue-blazed].

[K] 10.3 Descend into sag and turn left.

10.6 Descend steeply across rock slopes and below cliffs offering views of Shenandoah Valley.

11.2 Turn sharply left and continue descending.

[L] 11.7 Turn right onto Madison Run Fire Road [yellow-blazed].

[B] 12.3 Pass concrete post at Furnace Mtn Trail and continue on fire road past chain at Park Boundary.

[A] 12.6 Arrive back at parking area at end of fire road.

Hike No. 28
BLACKROCK

28

Length:	1.5 mi
Time Estimate:	45 min
Difficulty:	Easy
Elev. Change:	300 ft

Description: This short circuit offers an excellent opportunity to experience one of the Park's wilderness areas. Blackrock (3092 ft) is a tumbled mass of lichen-covered stone that offers spectacular views. Blackrock, like the other rocky slopes in this part of the Shenandoah, was once a huge cliff. Thousands of years ago the cliff crumbled and tumbled down the mountainside. The uneven surfaces that can be seen in the rocks were once cliff tops. The smooth surfaces indicate the places where the rock split.

Access: Park in paved area on west side of Skyline Drive approximately 0.6 mi south of MP 84.

Directions:
[A] 0.0 Walk around gate to concrete post at Trayfoot Mtn Trail [blue-blazed] and begin hike. Climb, soon level off, and then almost touch *AT*.
[B] 0.1 At concrete post at first spur trail, turn right. Then immediately turn left (south) onto *AT* [white-blazed].
[C] 0.4 Turn right onto Blackrock Spur Trail [blue-blazed] at concrete post and pass through interesting jumble of rocks. After passing through rocks, follow trail through wooded area.

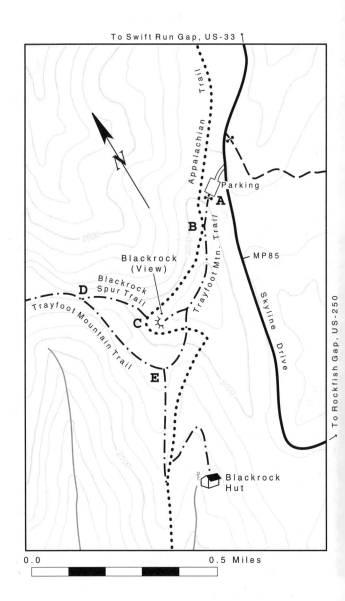

To Swift Run Gap, US-33

Appalachian Trail

Parking

A

B

Blackrock
(View)

Blackrock
Spur Trail

D

Trayfoot Mountain Trail

C

Trayfoot Mtn. Trail

E

MP 85

Skyline Drive

To Rockfish Gap, US-250

Blackrock
Hut

2500

0.0   0.5 Miles

[D] 0.7 At concrete marker, turn sharply left, almost doubling back, onto Trayfoot Mtn Trail [blue-blazed] and pass excellent views.

[E] 1.0 Turn left onto Blackrock Hut Service Road to stay on Trayfoot Mtn Trail.

1.1 Cross *AT* near top of ridge and continue on service road.

1.2 Reach ridge crest and continue on Trayfoot Mtn Trail.

1.4 Pass concrete post at Blackrock Spur Trail and continue on Trayfoot Mtn Trail.

[A] 1.5 Arrive back at parking area on Drive.

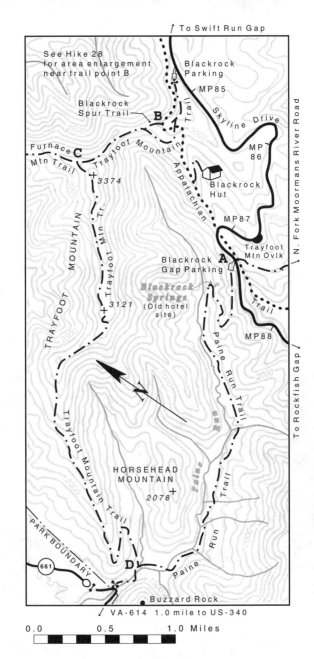

To Swift Run Gap

See Hike 28
for area enlargement
near trail point B

Blackrock
Parking
MP 85

Blackrock
Spur Trail

B

Furnace
Mtn Trail

C

Trayfoot Mountain Trail

3374

Appalachian Trail

Skyline Drive

MP 86

Blackrock
Hut

MP 87

Trayfoot
Mtn Ovlk

A

Blackrock
Gap Parking

*Blackrock
Springs*
(Old hotel
site)

N. Fork Moormans River Road

To Rockfish Gap

MP 88

Paine Run Trail

3121

TRAYFOOT MOUNTAIN

Trayfoot Mtn Tr.

Paine Run

HORSEHEAD
MOUNTAIN

2078

Trayfoot Mountain Trail

PARK BOUNDARY

661

D

Paine Run Trail

Paine Run

Buzzard Rock

VA-614 1.0 mile to US-340

0.0   0.5   1.0 Miles

Hike No. 29
TRAYFOOT MOUNTAIN

29

Length:	9.6 mi
Time Estimate:	6 hr
Difficulty:	Strenuous
Elev. Change:	2200 ft

Description: This hike begins at Blackrock Gap (2329 ft) and climbs on the Appalachian Trail to Blackrock (3092 ft), a tumbled mass of lichen-covered stone that offers spectacular year-round views. Then the hike climbs Trayfoot Mountain on a trail that follows an old fire road. After reaching the summit of Trayfoot Mountain (3374 ft), it descends along a ridge that offers many fine views to Paine Run, then climbs back to Blackrock Gap. (The trail between Trayfoot Mountain and Paine Run may be overgrown in summer.) This climb passes Buzzard Rock, a sharp peak, and the site of the former Blackrock Springs Hotel.

Access: Park at Blackrock Gap between MP 87 and MP 88 on Skyline Drive.

Directions:

[A] 0.0 Cross to east side of Drive and turn left (north) onto *AT* [white-blazed].

0.2 Cross Drive and stay on *AT*. Climb in old roadbed for 0.2 mi and then angle off slightly to left and parallel roadbed.

0.6 Enter old roadbed and bear left, uphill. In 100 ft, graded spur trail leads right, steeply downhill 0.2 mi to Blackrock Hut, which is deep in steep ravine. (Hut is for use by long-distance *AT* hikers only. Spring is located 30 ft in front of hut.) Continue past spur trail to right, away from trees, and climb long, steep grade along eastern side of ridge. (Old road runs parallel to trail on left.)

1.1 Cross Trayfoot Mtn Trail [blue-blazed] and continue on *AT*. In 300 ft, begin to circle Blackrock. This section of trail offers excellent year-round views.

[B] 1.2 Turn left onto Blackrock Spur Trail [blue-blazed] and descend.

1.4 Turn right onto Trayfoot Mtn Trail [blue-blazed] and climb Trayfoot Mtn.

[C] 2.0 Pass Furnace Mtn Trail [blue-blazed], which enters on right, and continue left to climb ridge on Trayfoot Mtn Trail.

2.1 Reach summit of Trayfoot Mtn. (Old road leads left to site of fire tower.) Descend gradually and ascend occasionally to cross several knobs. Both sides of trail offer views.

5.3 Reach switchback to left. Rocky ledge straight ahead offers excellent view of Buzzard Rock across Paine Run.

[D] 5.9 Turn right at Paine Run. In 50 ft, turn left and cross Paine Run onto Paine Run Trail [yellow-blazed]. Cross small stream in 100 ft and climb along Paine Run in bed of old fire road.

6.1 Cross main branch of Paine Run.

7.4 Cross stream.

8.7 Just after trail leaves run and makes sharp turn to right, Blackrock Springs and site of Blackrock Springs Hotel are a few hundred ft to left of trail. Continue climbing in old road bed.

[A] 9.6 Arrive back at Blackrock Gap Parking Area.

Hike No. 30
RIPRAP HOLLOW

30

Length:	9.5 mi
Time Estimate:	5 hr 45 min
Difficulty:	Moderate
Elev. Change:	2030 ft

Description: This circuit is exceptionally beautiful and passes through an interesting area of ecological succession that burned in 1990. The route passes excellent views at Calvary Rocks and Chimney Rocks and descends along Meadow Run through Cold Spring Hollow and Riprap Hollow. "Riprap" is the descriptive term for the broken rocks that are abundant in these hollows, which are among the few areas of the Park that contain Catawba rhododendron, a species which is common further south. The hollows also contain mountain laurel, fly poison, turkeybeard, starflower, and wild bleeding heart. (All of these flowers bloom in late May.) Meadow Run has an excellent swimming hole. Then the circuit climbs back via the Wildcat Ridge Trail. This circuit can be hiked from either the Wildcat Ridge Parking area or the Riprap Parking Area. Directions are provided from the Riprap Parking Area. **Note to backpackers:** These trails are heavily visited and legal campsites in Riprap Hollow are extremely limited.

Access from Riprap Parking Area: Park at Riprap Parking Area, a few ft north of MP 90 on west side of Skyline Drive.

Access from Wildcat Parking Area: Park at Wildcat Ridge Parking Area, just south of MP 92 on west side of Drive. Begin circuit at [E] on trail map. Hike 0.1 mi down Wildcat Ridge Trail [blue-blazed], turn right (north) onto *AT*, and follow circuit directions from [D].

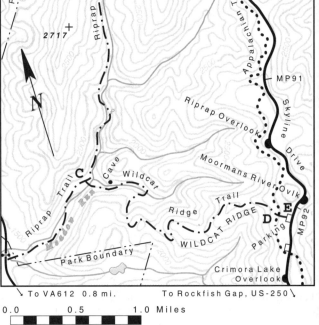

To Swift Run Gap, US-33

Chimney Rock

Calvary Rocks

B

ROCKS MOUNTAIN

+2945

Riprap Parking

A

MP90

Riprap Trail

Appalachian Trail

2717 +

N

MP91

Riprap Overlook

Skyline Drive

Moormans River Ovlk

Cave

Wildcat

C

Riprap Trail

Ridge Trail

WILDCAT RIDGE

D

E

MP92

Meadow Run

Park Boundary

Parking

Crimora Lake Overlook

To VA612 0.8 mi.

To Rockfish Gap, US-250

0.0   0.5   1.0 Miles

SOUTH DISTRICT

Directions:

[A] **0.0** From Riprap Parking Area, hike down spur trail about 100 ft to *AT* [white-blazed]. Turn right (north) onto *AT* and climb.

[B] **0.4** At summit of knob (2988 ft), turn left at concrete post onto Riprap Trail [blue-blazed]. Descend and then climb around Calvary Rocks.

1.4 Spur trail on right leads 15 ft to cliffs which offer excellent overlook near Calvary Rocks.

1.6 Turn sharply left where spur trail on right leads 75 ft to cliffs of Chimney Rock, which offer excellent views to north.

2.2 Stay on trail as it turns sharply left off ridge and descend into Cold Spring Hollow.

3.3 Pass series of small waterfalls, follow trail to right past sign, climb up and away from stream, and then descend.

3.5 Cross to east side of Meadow Run.

3.6 Pass deep pool at base of gentle waterfall (excellent swimming hole). Pink-blooming Catawba rhododendron grows along banks of run here. Then recross Meadow Run.

3.8 Pass through area on right slope that burned in 1990 forest fire.

[C] **4.2** Turn left at concrete post onto Wildcat Ridge Trail [blue-blazed], cross Meadow Run, and climb along small stream.

4.4 To left, across run, short spur trail leads to cave at base of cliffs.

4.5 Cross run, and in a few ft, at wooden sign, turn sharply right on switchback.

4.7 Recross run, then leave run and make moderate ascent.

5.1 Reach ridge line in sag and continue climbing along ridge. Ridge offers occasional views south to Turk Mtn. In winter Crimora Lake is visible below in Dorsey Hollow.

5.8 Trail levels near knob's summit (2514 ft).

[D] **6.8** Turn left (north) onto *AT* and continue through Catawba rhododendron on western side of ridge. (Wildcat Parking Area is 0.1 mi straight ahead at this turn.)

[A] **9.5** Turn right onto spur trail and arrive back at Riprap Trail Parking Area.

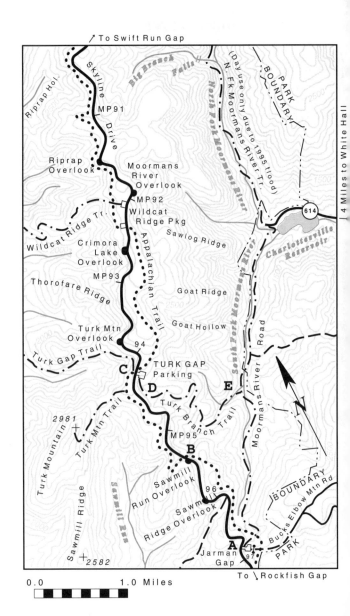

Hike No. 31
TURK BRANCH—
MOORMANS RIVER

31

Length:	7.8 mi (or 9.7 mi with side trip)
Time Estimate:	5 hr (or 6 hr 15 min with side trip)
Difficulty:	Moderate
Elev. Change:	2030 ft (or 2730 ft with side trip)

Description: This circuit starts at Jarman Gap, follows the Appalachian Trail north to Turk Gap, and then crosses Skyline Drive and descends to the South Fork of Moormans River. Then the circuit returns via Moormans River Road, which follows the original route of the Appalachian Trail to Jarman Gap. This circuit can be lengthened by taking a strongly recommended side trip to the summit of Turk Mountain (2981 ft), which offers outstanding views. The rock on the summit is a type of sandstone full of fossil worm holes, which give the rock a striated appearance. In mid May-early June, turkeybeard, a member of the lily family, blooms along the trail.

Access: Park at Jarman Gap, which is 0.3 mi north of MP 97 on Skyline Drive.

Directions:
A] **0.0** From Jarman Gap, pass chain across Moormans River Road [yellow-blazed] and descend.

0.1 Turn left (north) onto *AT* [white-blazed] and descend along west bank of Moormans River, which is just small creek here. Then leave creek and climb hill.

0.7 Partway up hill, cross over grass-covered pipeline.

1.2 Reach hill's summit. Bucks Elbow Mtn is visible to rear (east). Descend past views west to Turk Mtn, Sawmill Ridge, and outskirts of Waynesboro.

[B] **1.8** Cross Drive and begin climbing.

3.1 Reach summit of knob (2650 ft) and continue on *AT*.

3.2 Turk Mtn Trail [blue-blazed] enters on left.

To take side trip to Turk Mtn: Turn left onto Turk Mtn Trail, continue to summit, and then return via same trail (1.9 mi round trip).

To continue circuit: Continue north on *AT*. Cross Drive at Turk Gap (2625 ft).

[C] **3.4** Turn right at concrete post onto Turk Branch Trail [yellow-blazed], cross parking lot entrance, and parallel Drive.

[D] **3.7** Turn left to continue on Turk Branch Trail where unmarked trail goes right, uphill, to Drive. Trail is badly eroded in area of dying pines.

4.7 Cross stream. Trail improves as it enters hardwood forest. Cross stream three more times and descend.

[E] **5.9** Turn right onto Moormans River Road [yellow-blazed] and follow South Fork of Moormans River.

7.7 Cross *AT* and continue on Moormans River Road.

[A] **7.8** Arrive back at parking area at Jarman Gap.